SON OF CHARLEMAGNE

A Contemporary Life of Louis the Pious

Son of Charlemagne

A CONTEMPORARY LIFE OF
LOUIS THE PIOUS

ॐ

TRANSLATED, WITH INTRODUCTION AND NOTES BY

Allen Cabaniss

SYRACUSE UNIVERSITY PRESS

Library of Congress Catalog Card: 61-13987

COPYRIGHT © 1961 BY SYRACUSE UNIVERSITY PRESS

MANUFACTURED IN THE UNITED STATES OF AMERICA

BY THE COLONIAL PRESS INC., CLINTON, MASSACHUSETTS

For

Lisa Ann

Contents

SON OF CHARLEMAGNE

A Contemporary Life of Louis the Pious

Introduction

THE AUTHOR

The author of the book here presented for the first time in English translation is unknown by name, but even if a positive identification cannot be made, a reasonably clear picture of him arises from a study of his work. For instance, since he records the last moments and death of Emperor Louis[1] (which occurred on 20 June 840), he obviously survived his subject, but how much longer we do not know. He also records the death of a man whom we know from other accounts to have died in November 842.[2] Inasmuch as he learned about Louis's early life from 778 to 814 from a monk named Adhemar, "who," as he says, "being of the same age, was suckled with Louis," [3] it seems likely that our author was younger than the emperor. The high esteem in which Louis held him[4] indicates that he was not too much younger and his own invincible optimism[5] suggests that he was not elderly at the time of the emperor's death. Moreover, about the year 840, the age of sixty seems to him to be "burdensome old age." [6] A safe estimate therefore would probably place his birth about 800, making him the emperor's junior by twenty-two years. But this is quite frankly a conjecture, nothing more. The date of his death is even more uncertain. All we can say is that it was not

sooner than two or three years after the emperor's death
and burial. His nationality is also undetermined. Presumably
he was not a Goth[7] and probably not a Frank,[8] if we may
judge from the impersonal way in which he refers to both
of those peoples.

Since he tells us that he "was in the midst of palace
affairs,"[9] we assume that he was an intimate of the court
and we may suppose that he was a palatine official. There
is indeed other evidence in his treatise that he was often in
the emperor's entourage,[10] but in precisely what capacity
eludes us. Traditionally he has been deemed a court astronomer.[11] It is true that he exhibits a strong interest in
the stars and that his descriptions of celestial phenomena are
elaborate and detailed.[12] Of himself he states that he was
credited with knowledge of the subject and that the emperor
provided him with a place from which to make observations.[13]

But in a similar manner he displays strong interest in
medical science.[14] His physical analyses of the death of
Charlemagne and of Louis are very vivid, especially so in
the case of Louis.[15] He seems to lay stress upon exact descriptions of the ailments of Louis,[16] Lothair,[17] and Pope
Gregory IV.[18] At times he uses the language of disease to
characterize civil disorders in the realm.[19] Our author likewise demonstrates familiarity with law and legal procedure.[20] Once he distinguishes neatly between civil and "our"
law.[21] Still another important concern revealed by our
author is the weather,[22] occasionally depicted in unusually
graphic terms.[23]

His interest in astronomy, medicine, law and judicial
procedure, and weather, taken together, might simply suggest that he was a well-educated man. That fact is indeed

otherwise confirmed in ways to be mentioned below. But there remains a somewhat extraordinary interest, namely, in the details of military activities: preparations for war, sieges, precarious crossings of rivers, battle array, supplies and provisions, sea skirmishes, weapons, booty, pillaging.[24] Some of these passages are so vivid as to imply his presence as a participant, or at least as hanging on the words of an eye witness. He fairly revels in such matters and enlivens some of the accounts with direct discourse. In any case, the writer arises before us as a man of wide experience and manifold concerns.

Our author's style is neither elegant nor barbarous.[25] Occasionally he confuses the gender of words, employs the active voice for the passive, accusatives absolute instead of ablatives, the deponent as a passive, and the reflexive for oblique cases of the demonstrative pronoun. All in all, however, the style is clear, direct, and relatively simple. But it does convey evidence of some sophistication and learning. There are a few plays on words,[26] slight traces of irony,[27] several homely similes,[28] rhetorical questions,[29] and other such devices,[30] as well as dramatic exaggeration.[31] The most striking features are the effective use of direct discourse[32] and vivid descriptions.[33] And, as though to display virtuosity, the author indulges in what may be characterized as high-flown "purple patches." [34] He had certainly learned his art in a school. Further evidence of his study lies in his use of good sources, of which, like a true scholar, he informs us. These will be discussed later.[35]

The Anonymous was a sincere admirer of Emperor Louis,[36] but not a blind one. He was, of course, an imperialist: to him Louis never ceased to be the emperor, even during the two brief intervals when Lothair held the actual reins of government. Louis was right, and his sons and their followers were wrong, during the two rebellions. Yet the emperor, however mild, is depicted as utterly human. Our author gives no such idealized portrait of him as Thegan did, or as Einhard did of Charlemagne. Louis was indeed precocious as a child, just in his dealings, and pious in his religious practices, but also a very ardent sportsman who permitted nothing to interfere with his regular seasons of hunting (and fishing).[37]

There is an interesting ambivalence in the attitude of the Anonymous toward churchmen. He was certainly respectful and somewhat religious, but he was by no means subservient to ecclesiastical officials. There seems to be in him perhaps a strain of what may be called "anticlericalism":[38] a scorn for monks who "hide away in anxiety" for their own salvation,[39] a cynical belief that accession to the papacy might be a fall downward instead of a leap upward,[40] a puritanical abhorrence of proud prelates displaying worldly pomp,[41] a feeling that even a pope could be excommunicated if he violated the canons,[42] and a disgust with time-serving bishops.[43] It is an impressive array of subtle remarks which betray his deeply felt sentiments.

His profound imperialism and his apparent "anticlericalism" arouse a suspicion that the Anonymous was a representative of that rare early-medieval phenomenon, the literate layman. But that attractive possibility we must, I suppose, set aside, although his citations of Scripture could be interpreted as strengthening it. There are only nine direct quotations and sixteen partial quotations or allusions[44] (not all of them certain)—a relatively small number, considering the length of his treatise. Six of the latter may be properly discounted, since they are either verbally imprecise or so brief as to be accidental.[45] Nine of the others seem to be introduced quite casually, some out of context, as though to brighten an utterly commonplace statement.[46] The remaining one mentions Scripture, but cites only the Four Cardinal Virtues which could as easily have been derived from a pagan source.[47] Turning to the direct quotations, we discover that three of them also are brief moralistic statements which serve merely to improve an ordinary remark.[48] Four others are introduced sententiously and aphoristically to soothe the readers or the emperor.[49] Still another immediately follows quotation of the ancient pagan maxim, "Nothing to excess." [50] The last one, although basically a Scriptural verse, is actually the Introit of Mass for the fourth Sunday in Lent (called Mid-Lent or Laetare). It is moreover cited not as Scripture but as the "ecclesiastical *cantilena* of the Office [Introit]." [51]

Not one of the quotations or allusions is doctrinal or theological. Of the nine direct quotations, only three are from the New Testament, and they are minor proverbial sayings, one even derived by the New Testament writer from a pagan source.[52] The remaining ones are from Job, Jeremiah (two passages), Wisdom, Ecclesiasticus, and Isaiah (or rather, the Liturgy).[53] Of nine allusions (ignoring the six which may be accidental),[54] five are from the New Testament,[55] only three of which are of any significance.[56] Apparently our author employed the Bible simply as a source of proverbial sayings without theological import.[57] We may therefore hazard the guess that the Anonymous was formally religious, by no means excessively pious, and quite laic in outlook. This presumption seems to be strengthened by his omission of reference to the Jews. Considering the prominence of those religionists at the court and the hostility provoked against them,[58] to ignore them appears to be an instance of sovereign indifference to religious matters.

To summarize, we find the Anonymous to be a man, neither Frank nor Goth, born about A.D. 800, a devoted palace functionary of some sort, with great admiration for the emperor and apparently with an "anticlerical" bent; well-trained and interested in astronomy, medicine, jurisprudence, meteorology, military science, as well as in grammar and historical research; moralistic and conventionally religious; modestly frank, generally unsuperstitious, full of common sense and sedate cheerfulness. It is extremely regrettable that we cannot identify him,[59] but to attempt to do so would be the merest guess. If only Fridugis had lived long enough, I would have pointed to him as the author. The viewpoint suits him precisely, but, alas, he died in 830.

There is another question even more tantalizing than the one respecting identification. It is, "How was the identity of such a man as we have described lost?" It is as unanswerable as the other. We can scan the list of persons known to have frequented the imperial court of Louis the Pious, many of them quite famous (or notorious), others mere names. We cannot find our author. Yet we know that somewhere in that group once stood a man, nameless and shadowy to us, but to them the veriest of realities, respected, learned, half-detached, dependable, and loyal.

THE SUBJECT

Later generations have consistently proclaimed the inferiority of Louis the Pious to his illustrious father. Evidence of that attitude lies in the proliferation of serious studies, as well as an incredible amount of legendary materials, about the great Charles and the relative paucity of works about

Louis. Yet in the ninth century Charles was the subject of only one important biography, while his son was the subject of four.[60] From the literary standpoint, therefore, Louis was deemed his father's equal, if not indeed his superior. Furthermore, in spite of his acknowledged greatness, Charles was at least twice after his death depicted as suffering the torments of hell or purgatory,[61] while Louis was never so portrayed. Some of the elder courtiers even thought Louis's reign as glorious as the reign of King Pepin, his grandfather, curiously omitting from consideration the reign of Charlemagne.[62] In his own lifetime Louis evoked more obvious loyalty and hatred than his father had done, that is, within the empire (unless we suppose that his father systematically suppressed all dissident expression). Charles's name was known and feared farther afield than was his son's, yet Louis's control was just as effective from beyond the Elbe to the Ebro, from Rome to the North Sea.

It is true that Louis was not a "founder" as his father and grandfather were. But it is only an accident of history that his partitioning (and hence dissolution) of the Carolingian state was successful. Both his father and grandfather had arranged for similar divisions, but death had countered the execution of their schemes. Consequently Louis cannot be truly reckoned as a "destroyer." It was his fate to be overshadowed on the one hand by the might and glamor of Charlemagne and on the other by the unworthy bickerings, ambitions, and aims of his sons. A well-known university press has advertised future publication of editions of Einhard's *Vita Karoli* and Nithard's *De dissensionibus filiorum Ludovici pii* in these words: "The most famous of all medieval biographies, to which the Chronicle of Nithard is, in effect, a sequel." [63] The statement is partially true, but the implication is entirely gratuitous, for it virtually suppresses the more than quarter of a century between Charles's death and the battle of Fontenoy. In spite of discontent and revolts, Louis proved capable of preserving the heritage received from his father in 814 and in stabilizing the tensions of party strife until his own death in 840. That was task enough for any man, and by ordinary (perhaps extraordinary) standards a not immodest success.

Louis has also suffered from the epithets attached to his name, "the Debonair" and "the Pious." The latter has been the more customary, especially among Germanic-speaking students (including English); the former occasionally employed particularly by French-speaking students. *Debonair* suggests "good-natured to the point of weakness." Our Anonymous shows in numerous instances that Louis was both mild and stern. "To one fault alone he was deemed to have succumbed," says our author, "namely, that he was too mild." [64] And "that man of mercy" he called him,[65] one who did not exult over the death of his enemies.[66] Examples of this kindness occur in the commutation of death sentences to banishment, tonsure, or degradation from rank.[67] It appears also in an almost pathological reaction to those who disliked him.[68] Sometimes, however, the expression of magnanimity had a hypocritical quality, as when Louis showed unwonted clemency to hostile Saxons and Frisians, but only to bind them to him in alliance,[69] and when he pardoned the rebellious Basques, but only because their possessions had already been destroyed.[70]

By the time our author wrote, the good nature of Louis was apparently an already established tradition. But even as the Anonymous yielded to that tradition, he found that he had apologetically to modify it. Four notable illustrations may be cited. First, "although by nature very mild," [71] Louis callously expelled his sisters from court, "even though they did not deserve such treatment." [72] Second, in an overwrought condition, Louis once condemned to blinding a certain Tullius, "who seemed almost worthy of pardon." [73] Third, in spite of his attribute of reverence, Louis in 833 treated Pope Gregory IV "less fittingly than was appropriate" [74] simply because the pontiff was not one of his partisans. Fourth, even on his deathbed he displayed such churlishness toward his son, Louis of Bavaria, that the prelates in attendance were not edified by his disposition, nor were they successful in effecting a sincere reconciliation. [75]

Indeed, there were occasions when Louis seemed to exhibit real cruelty. He waged "total war" with all the unnecessary suffering which that entails. He allowed his soldiers to cut and burn fields of grain[76] and received "gladly" reports of devastation.[77] Foemen who had come for a conference under terms of truce were seized and burned alive.[78] Women and children were captured and held as hostages.[79] The use of torture was permitted.[80] The crowning brutality was the merciless treatment of his own youthful nephew, Bernard, king of Italy. Bernard had surrendered voluntarily and acknowledged his recreancy. He was nonetheless condemned to death. But Louis, "acting more indulgently," as our author observes, altered the sentence to blinding, and Bernard, since he did not calmly acquiesce in this outrage, "brought bitter death upon himself." [81] Even Louis had later to confess and do penance for this unmerited harshness, although the Anonymous states that he acted voluntarily.[82]

There were other lesser characteristics which tempered Louis's "mildness." As brother after brother died, Louis began to feel his spirit rise as his fortunes rose and "the hope of a world to be gained surged up in him." [83] We ordinarily call that feeling avarice or ambition or perhaps pride. When retainers advised him to go to his ailing father, Louis delayed, shrewdly guessing that it would be more politic to wait for an official summons.[84] That decision we can hardly call filial devotion. Still further, since it suited his purpose to have people friendly to him at that critical moment, he "was cheerfully indulgent to those seeking peace whom he had been accustomed to weary with warfare." [85] And that is an illustration of what we pejoratively call prudential ethics. Impatience appeared in Louis when something happened to exasperate his mind which was "usually very mild." [86] A tendency to be pompous is reflected in his high-flown remarks about Halley's comet.[87] And obvious injustice was the result of his dealing with his grandsons, the sons of the late Pepin of Aquitaine.[88] All in all, good-natured kindness was none too unmitigated in Louis the Pious.

The related charge of weakness is more serious. Yet to have commanded such loyalty as to be capable of overcoming the massive revolts of his sons indicates strength, not weakness. Some students have painted Emperor Louis as supinely yielding to the influence of his wives, especially Judith, or Count Bernard of Barcelona, or of the church, or of others. Professor F. L. Ganshof states: "It should be noted that Louis the Pious seems to have needed the constant and authoritative advice of a strong personality"; and he names six such persons: Benedict of Aniane, Wala, Helisachar, Fridugis, Hilduin, and Matfrid.[89] In this *Vita*, however, the emperor is always shown as the master of most situations, or if heeding another it is usually the manly

voice of his illegitimate half-brother, Drogo.[90] In fact, some
of the most touching scenes in the book have Drogo in the
background.[91]

Far more devastating has been the consequence of Louis's
designation as "the Pious." Devout and religious he undoubtedly was, but in no wise a mere creature of monks,
bishops, or pope. So much will be evident in the pages of
the Anonymous, but Louis was by no means the puritan he
has been pictured.[92] There are several facts to be stressed
here. Louis's first marriage is said by our Anonymous
(perhaps inadvertently) to have been undertaken for fear
that the emperor "might be dragged into the manifold toils
of lust by the natural heat of the body," [93] an assertion
which implies that the peril had not been entirely avoided
and lends credence to the possibility that his daughter
Alpaïs or Elpheid may have been illegitimate.[94] Moreover,
the account of the selection of Judith as his second wife[95]
suggests that Louis had an eye for a pretty face and a comely
form. In any case, he chose a prize that was universally
recognized as attractive (if one favored the court-party),
or as seductive and alluring (if one favored the anti-court
faction).[96] That is not to say, of course, that many a real
Puritan has not made the same choice and for the same
reason, but the action is not usually deemed characteristic
of the kind.

Too much has been made of Thegan's approving report
that Louis despised the old heathen heroic songs which he
had learned in his youth and that he never raised his voice
in a loud guffaw or "showed his white teeth in a smile."
The passage is worth quoting in full:

Never did Louis raise his voice in laughter, not even at
high festivals when strolling musicians and actors, jesters

and mimes, flute-players or guitarists appeared at his table for the entertainment of the people. While the people were laughing at the grotesquerie in his presence, even then he never showed his white teeth in a smile.[97]

It should be particularly observed that although the emperor did not join in the general merriment, there was and continued to be ample opportunity for not too innocent amusement at court, which the emperor, for all his piety, made no effort to repress.

"Pious" though Louis was, even "most pious," his court was not that bright and shining standard of Christian orthodoxy which the epithet might intimate. Bodo, a contemporary, has stated that while he was a palatine official he actually observed among the other retainers as many as fourteen men holding as many variant religious opinions and practices. Whether that was absolutely accurate is of little concern, but the fact that such a report could be made and believed is significant. This informant went still further and charged that the Christianity he had known at court was nothing but idolatry. He may have been too rash in his remarks, but again the fact that even one man high in official circles could deliver such a judgment makes one suspect that the imperial environment was not entirely unreprehensible. There is indeed some confirmation of Bodo's criticisms, not, to be sure, only among constant attendants at Aachen, but also among those receiving the favor of the administration. Hilduin and Einhard were superstitiously attached to the cult of relics; Amalarius, erstwhile bishop of Trèves, was indulging more or less uninhibitedly in heretical interpretations of the Liturgy; and others were resorting to large-scale manifestations of ancestral paganism.

A more dangerous attitude of indifference to conventional Christianity was the approval given to Judaism. Our informant in the preceding paragraph is an apt illustration. In 839, while he was a royal deacon, Bodo abandoned Christianity for Judaism, changing his name to Eleazar. But his act was only a dramatic climax to something which had been going on for a score of years or more. As early as the 820's, Carolingian grandees were bypassing their Christian clerics and going to Jewish rabbis for prayers and blessings. Businessmen shifted their market day from Saturday to Sunday because so many persons preferred to attend synagogue instead of church. And all that apparently without the slightest protest from the court. Only a few disgruntled bishops were aroused. In fact the women of the court were showering gifts upon the women of the Jewish community as demonstrations of favor. Heinrich Graetz calls the days of Louis the Pious "a golden age for the Jews . . . , such as they had never enjoyed, and were destined never again to enjoy in Europe." [98]

In addition to latitudinarian religious expression, common fame attributed gross and shameful immoralities to the court of the pious Louis. If we may cite Bodo again, he boasted that as a palatine cleric he had often seduced women in the very precincts of Charlemagne's cathedral at Aachen. Agobard, an enemy of the palace, spoke of sordid filth, crimes, and evil factions there. Still further, he claimed that a majority of the people of the realm and its dependencies knew and jested obscenely about the cuckolded emperor. Somewhat later, Paschasius Radbertus wrote about the revelry that turned day into night, night into day, and shattered all vestiges of virtue. For him and his readers the palace was a brothel where adultery was queen and an adulterer king.

Whatever the value of these exaggerated rumors, they twice proved the ostensible reason for large-scale, though vain, revolts.[99]

Most credible of all the gossip, however, was the whispering campaign that some forms of witchcraft or black magic were being cultivated at court. Pachasius declared that the palace had become a theater where such delusions and enormities were streaming from the hands of sorceresses, such abominations were being pursued, as he had supposed were no longer practiced anywhere in the whole world.[100] Unwittingly our anonymous author tends to confirm this charge. First, he admits that the revolt of 830 was in part based on belief that Louis the Pious was a victim of "certain delusions" (*quibusdam praestigiis elusum*) which deprived him of reason and which therefore required the desperate intervention of his sons.[101] Secondly, he records along with others that at the fall of Châlon in 834 the retreating forces of Lothair captured and tried the nun Gerberga as a witch (*venefica*) and executed her by drowning in hideous parody of the ordeal by cold water.[102] This point is of consequence when we recall that Gerberga was a sister of Count Bernard of Barcelona, the most favored man at court. Thirdly, in the description of Louis's death, the Anonymous states that the emperor's last words were, "Avaunt! Avaunt!" as though he had seen an evil spirit.[103] It is unusually ironic that the dying utterance of the "most pious" Louis should be a formula of exorcism.

In view of the evidence presented in the six preceding paragraphs, it will be clear that the "piety" of Louis has, by late-Christian moral and religious standards, been severely overdrawn. We cannot, of course, rid him of his traditional epithet, however much we might like to do so, but we must rid ourselves of the modern connotations of the word (as we have apparently done in the case of *pius Aeneas*).

THE BOOK AND ITS VALUE

"Whether he was a competent astronomer, I would not say; but he was certainly not a competent historian," says one writer.[104] "This is history and not a political tract; and the author can write Latin, even if his style is somewhat ornate," says another.[105] With these two observations we are in the midst of a difference of opinion about the value of our anonymous *Vita Hludovici*. The question is in reality not one but three. Is the book reliable? Is it original? Is it artistic?

We should first recognize that in Parts I and III the chronology is somewhat erratic. A few examples may be cited. Chapter 10, for instance, recounts the imperial coronation of Charlemagne in Rome, which, as we know, occurred on Christmas day, 800.[106] Chapter 11, opening with the words, "Later, when summer was burgeoning . . . ," refers to the conclusion of the thirty-three-year-old Saxon campaign which ended in 804.[107] Thereupon, chapter 12, beginning, "The winter having passed . . . ," reverts to the events of the year 800 and the succeeding chapter very properly deals with 801. Chapter 13 then passes to affairs of 809, omitting the intervening years. The exceedingly tangled chronology of chapters 55-61 is dealt with below in appropriate Notes which need not be here repeated. Significantly enough, Part II has little or no such aberrations. Can the book then be deemed reliable? If it is used alone, the answer is a qualified negative in respect of chronology, although as indicated it is only in eleven chapters out of sixty-four that serious dislocations occur. Fortunately there exist controls by which to correct the Anonymous and, apart from the question of dates, the author is not at sharp variance from other accounts of the time. Proper adjustment is made in the Notes to the text below.

Of greater concern has been the question about the book's independence, one scholar asserting dogmatically that "it is not a work of any originality." [108] The author himself, as noted earlier, mentions three distinct sources of his treatise: first, a narrative (probably written, now lost) of a monk named Adhemar, dealing with the period from the birth of Louis in 778 to his accession in 814; second, his own observation; and third, that which he had been able to ascertain, since he was at times associated with the court.[109] The last is quite probably an allusion to the *Annales regni Francorum* which underlie Part II involving the years 814–829. His own direct observation relates apparently to the last decade of Louis's life and reign, 830–840.

A study of the *Vita Hludovici* reveals also a reliance on Einhard's *Vita Karoli* and either on other annals, such as the *Annales Bertiniani*, or more likely on the immediate sources of such annals. It also reveals that there are indeed matters derived from the author's own observation and from verbal reports of other intimates of the court. The Anonymous has, in popular language, "laid his cards on the table." The interesting point is that Part II, in which dependence on the royal annals is most obvious, is more accurate and orderly in its dating of events than Part I which rests on Adhemar's account and Part III which relies most heavily on the writer's experience.

But there is a further question: did the Anonymous also rely on other lives of Louis the Pious, namely, the poem of Ermoldus Nigellus, Thegan's biography and its brief continuation, and Book I of Nithard's treatise concerning the strife of Louis's sons? Virtually all scholars eliminate Thegan from consideration. Some, however, believe that use was made of Ermoldus Nigellus[110] and of Nithard.[111] So far as the time element is involved the former could be true; Ermoldus wrote between 826 and 830, and our Anonymous wrote after 842. There is moreover some evidence to indicate that our author knew the poem, so we can in all likelihood add the poem as a source. Concerning the use of Nithard, one scholar goes so far as to claim that the Anonymous was merely a plagiarist,[112] but this charge has been amply and satisfactorily refuted.[113] On the contrary, the reverse has been, I believe, conclusively demonstrated,[114] so conclusively indeed that I shall not summarize the arguments. I shall add but one remark. The most noteworthy similarity between the Anonymous and Nithard is the following. The *Vita Hludovici*, chapter 61, states: "quicquid regni trans Rhenum fuit, sibi vindicandum statuit." Nithard, *De dissensionibus* . . . , I, 6, states: "quicquid trans Rhenum regni continebatur, sibi vindicare vellet." Neither author was necessarily citing the other; both may have been using a common source. In fact the language of the *Annales Bertiniani*, *anno* 838, "habitaque secus quam oportuerat conflictatione verborum, quicquid ultra citraque Renum paterni iuris usurpaverat . . . ," suggests that in the "conflict of words" the very words were of supreme importance and hence were deeply impressed upon everyone who came to know about them (as, to be sure, the *Annales Bertiniani* indicate).

In the sense that a historical treatise relies upon evidence, it is not and cannot be strictly original. It may be original only if it presents evidence not found elsewhere or at least

not found in the usual places. By this definition our anonymous *Vita* is clearly "original." It is, for instance, our only
source of information about the childhood and youth of
Emperor Louis and of his government as king of Aquitaine.
There is no need to recapitulate all the eighteen places at
which the Anonymous gives us our only information or
information fuller and clearer than other sources.[115] It will
be sufficient merely to mention that only the *Vita Hludovici*
records the birth of Charles the Bald, the place of Adalard's
exile, the banishment of Louis's sisters, and the name of
Einhard as the one securing the relics of Saints Marcellinus
and Peter from Rome.[116]

The anonymous life is then, with reservations, generally
reliable and sufficiently original; it remains only to inquire
into its artistry, if any. After a brief but adequate Prologue, the book is divided into sixty-four chapters, which in
turn may be grouped into three Parts of almost equal
length: Part I, twenty chapters; Part II, twenty-three; and
Part III, twenty-one. The first Part deals with the first
thirty-six years of Louis's life; the second, with the next
sixteen; and the third, with the last ten. Such division is
quite realistic and is approximately what a modern historian
would make.

The apt allusions to and citations of ancient and Biblical
authors are mentioned in the Notes below or in this Introduction, as are the direct discourse, plays on words, use of
irony, rhetorical questions and statements, dramatic exaggeration, homely similes, purple passages, and so forth. One
of the most precious descriptions is that of the seven-year-
old boy as he met his father at Paderborn: in Basque garb,
with round mantle, long, flowing sleeves, full trousers, boots
and spurs, with dart in his hand, and on horseback.[117] An-

other is the peculiarly graphic story of an attack on Tortosa in 810: the construction of prefabricated boats to cross the Ebro, the Indian-like traveling by night, hiding in forests by day, and the shrewd Moorish detection of the stratagem.[118] Still another is the excellent account of the apparition of Halley's comet in 837, to which is added a strikingly intimate passage concerning the relation between emperor and author (presented in direct discourse).[119] The total eclipse of the sun in 840 is also depicted in a vivid manner.[120] Throughout the work a feeling of warmth is achieved by the delicate employment of the first person singular, which the writer uses quite modestly, almost imperceptibly, yet often enough to preserve the sense of immediacy. By late-Classical technical standards Einhard's *Vita Karoli* may be the superior work, but the anonymous *Vita Hludovici* is by far the more entertaining, as indeed the more reliable.

This book and the conditions of life portrayed in it seem to be in some manner a definite stage in the emergence of the high-medieval code of chivalry out of the old Germanic practice. Four elements appear deserving of special, though brief, comment: an emphasis on warlike qualities, the importance of the oath, a sensitive regard for honor, and the prominence of ceremonious actions. The first two are Germanic characteristics especially noted by Tacitus in his *Germania*.[121] The third is closely related to them, while the fourth is at least not foreign to them but it may be derived from late-imperial practice.

Throughout the *Vita* there are recurrent references not only to war itself, but also to the warlike sport of hunting. Year after year, springtime and autumn, the Anonymous recorded that the emperor spent seasons of hunting "after the manner of the Franks" [122] or "according to the custom

of Frankish kings." [123] Nothing apparently interfered with
this exercise, whether a serious accident twenty days
earlier,[124] defection of allies,[125] or insurrection.[126] Once in
pious vein the author stated that care of the churches was
emperor's "pastime and sport," [127] but how wrong the
author was is obvious from his own evidence. The particular kind of hunting is not specified, although occurring as
it did in mountainous and forested regions (for example, the
Ardennes and the Vosges), it must have been the chase of
wild animals. Falconry, however, is alluded to in one instance.[128]

Knightly combat, specifically identified as Germanic, was
another evidence of warlike activity. One instance is re-
counted in some detail; others are merely mentioned. In the
year 820 the count of Barcelona (Bera) was charged with
disloyalty. He challenged his accuser (Sanila) to a judicial
duel. They met on horseback, "according to their own law
since each was a Goth." [129] A later count of Barcelona
(Bernard), similarly accused, offered to submit the case to
like adjudication, but the accuser, refusing to appear, de-
faulted.[130] The importance of the warrior-quality is still
further emphasized by the stress placed on the girding of a
youth with the sword. At the tender age of three or four,
Louis was, for the sake of the symbol, armed and placed on
a horse.[131] Later, at the age of twelve, he was formally
invested with his sword as the sign of his coming of age.
In the very following year he accompanied his brother,
Pepin of Italy, on a campaign against Beneventum.[132] Long
afterward, in 838, Louis girded his own fifteen-year-old son
Charles with the sword and other weapons as a sign of
maturity.[133]

The significance of the oath is presented in many refer-

ences. There are two kinds recorded, the oath of purgation
and of fealty. The former appears, for example, in the case
noted immediately above. When Count Bernard's accuser
refused the challenge to judicial combat, the count cleared
himself by oath.[134] In 831 Queen Judith in like manner
cleared herself of charges.[135] The oath of fealty followed
Charles's assumption of the sword, also alluded to above.[136]
Much earlier, Chorso had been "bound by the bonds of
oaths." [137] But that example also illustrates the weakness of
such bonds when not accompanied by forceful sanctions.
In part, such sanctions were imposed by the exchange of
hostages.[138]

In the situation marked by warlikeness and oaths, it is
obvious that a sense of honor would be worn on the sleeve.
And so it was in the days of our anonymous author. Guile
was a blot on the escutcheon to be avenged.[139] External
plainness and need brought disgrace upon a person.[140] Ac-
cusations must be met by force of arms or by solemn purgation, not by legal disproof.[141] Closely related is the valuation
put on ceremonious procedure. Permission to leave is mentioned frequently by the Anonymous. To depart without
congé was an affront.[142] Even in the face of danger, permission must be sought. Admission to an audience was
another ceremony which was necessary even in (to us)
strange circumstances: the queen had to secure formal "leave
to speak more privately" with the emperor, although he was
her husband.[143] Like amenities must be observed even between enemies. Conversation had about it a courtliness which
seems so pompous today, if we may generalize from the
discussion about Halley's comet.[144] The author was aware
that some things could be said, while others could not. Yet
the emperor, observing this discretion, supposed that he

could read the mind of the student of astronomy. Each then resorted to Scriptural quotations or platitudes.

At that time also commendation or the oath of fealty involved the ceremony of placing one's hands in the hands of his lord. It seems to be implied when Wala acquiesced in Louis's accession and commended himself to Louis "according to the custom of the Franks." [145] It is clearly stated that Harold (Heriold) of the Danes entrusted himself to Louis's hands "according to the custom of the Franks." [146] Similar was the case when young Charles was invested with Neustria: the grandees of the province "gave their hands to Charles." [147]

The most elaborate ceremony, however, was the reception of the pope.[148] An honor guard was dispatched to accompany the pontiff. His arrival was greeted by a procession of clergy followed by the emperor on foot. The emperor acted as the pope's squire when the prelate dismounted. A conference and Mass consumed the first day. On the second the emperor tendered a sumptuous banquet and dowered the pope with numerous gifts. On the third day the pope reciprocated. It was not until the fourth day that the business for which the meeting was arranged was transacted.

From the preceding remarks one can almost visualize a society as portrayed in the later *chansons*. War was the main function. When war was not being fought, warlike exercises were provided. Society was based on "a man's word," easily broken but generally quite sufficient. Honor was the most ostensible virtue of that society, to be maintained at all costs and to be avenged when offended. Above all, the amenities were to be preserved, clothing the life of the times, at least superficially, in a leisurely, courtly habit. We know, of course, from this *Vita* itself, as well as from other

contemporary literature, that the appearance was deceptive,
that many uncourteous things happened and that haste was
often necessary, but the illusion is there nonetheless.

BIBLIOGRAPHY

In attempting to assemble a modern bibliography respecting Louis the Pious, one is again impressed by the wealth of
works on his father, the considerable number of treatises
on his successors, and the incredible paucity of materials
about him. There are, for example, the valuable recent
studies by A. J. Kleinclausz, *Charlemagne* (Paris: Hachette,
1934); *Éginhard* (Paris: Société d'édition "Les belles lettres,"
1942); and *Alcuin* (Paris: Société d'édition "Les belles
lettres," 1948); by Louis Halphen, *Études critiques sur
l'histoire de Charlemagne* (Paris: Alcan, 1921; to be read
with W. Levison's strictures in mind, on which see his
review in *Neues Archiv für ältere deutsche Geschichtskunde*, XLV [1924], 390–94), and *Charlemagne et l'empire
carolingien* (Paris: Michel, 1947); and by Joseph Calmette,
*L'effrondrement d'un empire et la naissance d'une Europe
IXe-Xe siècles* (Paris: Aubier, 1941); *Charlemagne, sa vie
et son oeuvre* (Paris: Michel, 1945); and *Charlemagne*
(Paris: Presses Universitaires de France, 1951). These are
only a few of the veritable flood of books dealing with the
period before and after Louis the Pious, but which, of
course, throw light on his reign.

An old study by Robert Dorr, *De bellis Francorum cum
Arabibus gestis usque ad obitum Karoli Magni* (Königsberg:
Inaugural-Dissertation, 1861), especially pages 51 to 57, is
important for our purpose since it employs part of the
anonymous *Vita Hludovici*. The antiquated works by Friedrich Funck, *Ludwig der Fromme: Geschichte der Auflösung*

des grossen Frankenreichs (Frankfurt a/M, 1832), A. Himly, *Louis le débonnaire et Wala* (Paris: Firmin Didot Frères, 1849), and Rudolf Foss, *Ludwig der Fromme vor seiner Thronbesteigung* (Berlin: Progr. d. Friedr.-Wilh.-Gymn., 1858), have been largely superseded by Bernhard Simson, *Jahrbücher des fränkischen Reichs unter Ludwig dem Frommen*, 2 vols. (Leipzig: Duncker und Humblot, 1874, 1876). This last is the fundamental study. It begins, however, with the year 814 (Louis's accession). There is a brief note by J. Girgensohn, "Zum Astronomus," *Forschungen zur deutschen Geschichte*, XV (1875), 653–55, and an interesting sketch by F. L. Ganshof, "Louis the Pious Reconsidered," *History, XLII*, No. 149 (Oct. 1957), 171–80. The chapter by Réné Poupardin, "Louis the Pious," *Cambridge Medieval History*, III (New York: Macmillan, 1924), 1–22, turns out to be hardly more than a severely abridged translation of the anonymous *Vita*. Above all there is Walther Nickel, *Untersuchungen über die Quellen, den Wert und den Verfasser der Vita Hludovici des "Astronomus"* (Potsdam: Edmund Stein, 1919), a fifty-two-page "Inaugural-Dissertation zur Erlangung der Doktorwürde genehmigt von der Philosophischen Fakultät der Friedrich-Wilhelms-Universität zu Berlin." Brief though it is, it is packed with the most substantial information. Some of the arguments are challenged (but I do not believe successfully) by M. Buchner, "Entstehungszeit und Verfasser der Vita Hludowici des Astronomen," *Historisches Jahrbuch*, LX (1940), 14–45.

For our purpose, the works of Max Manitius are invaluable, in particular his *Geschichte der lateinischen Literatur des Mittelalters*, I (Munich: Beck, 1911); his "Zu dem Epos 'Karolus Magnus et Leo Papa,'" *Neues Archiv der Gesellschaft für ältere deutsche Geschichtskunde*, IX (1884),

614–19; and his "Zu deutschen Geschichtsquelle des 9 bis 12
Jahrhunderts," *ibid.*, XI (1886), 45–73. Substance is still to
be derived from Adolf Ebert, *Allgemeine Geschichte der
Literatur des Mittelalters im Abendlande*, II (Leipzig: Vogel,
1880). A fine discussion and an excellent bibliography are
to be found in Heinz Löwe, *Die Karolinger vom Tode
Karls des Grossen bis zum Vertrag von Verdun* (Heft III
of Wattenbach-Levison, *Deutschlands Geschichtsquellen im
Mittelalter;* Weimar: Hermann Böhlaus Nachfolger, 1957),
335–38. Of value are P. Fournès, *Étude critique sur la vie
de Louis le Pieux par Thégan et l'Astronome* (Paris, 1907),
and H. Kuhn, *Das literarische Porträt Ludwigs des Frommen*
(Basel: diss., 1930).

The wary researcher is kept from many a chronological
slip by Johann Friedrich Böhmer, Engelbert Mühlbacher,
Johann Lechner, *Die Regesten des Kaiserreichs unter den
Karolingern 751–918* (Innsbruck: Verlag der Wagner'schen
Universitäts-Buchhandlung, 1908), and P. B. Gams, *Series
episcoporum ecclesiae catholicae* (reprint; Graz: Akademische Druck- und Verlagsanstalt, 1957). Theodor von
Oppolzer, *Canon der Finsternisse* (Vienna: Karl Gerold's
Sohn, 1887), permits us to check dates by allusions to
eclipses of sun and moon. On the comets mentioned by
medieval historians, a modern scientific control is afforded
by F. Baldet and G. de Obaldia, *Catalogue général des
orbites de comètes de l'an 466 à 1952* (Paris: Centre National
de la Recherche Scientifique, 1952).

On many details of the period, we can profitably consult
J. Calmette, *De Bernardo sancti Guillelmi filio (?–844)*
(Toulouse: Privat, 1902); and for excellent interpretation,
Heinrich Fichtenau, *Das karolingische Imperium* (Zürich:
Fretz und Wasmuth, 1949). Two works contemporary with

our anonymous *Vita* have appeared in fairly recent editions: Ermold le Noir, *Poème sur Louis le Pieux et Epitres au Roi Pépin,* ed. and trans. Edmond Faral (Paris: Champion, 1932), and Nithard, *Histoire des fils de Louis le Pieux,* ed. and trans. Ph. Lauer (Paris: Champion, 1926), both in the series, "Les classiques de l'histoire de France au moyen âge." The former should be studied with the remarks by Chaim Tykocinski, *Quellenkritische Beiträge zur Geschichte Ludwig des Frommen* (Leipzig: Schmidt, 1898), part of a longer thesis on "Ermoldus Nigellus und sein Gedicht"; the latter, with the masterful treatment by Gerold Meyer (von Knonau), *Ueber Nithard vier Bücher Geschichten* (Leipzig: Hirzel, 1866).

Not many MSS of the *Vita Hludovici* are extant, if indeed many ever existed: one of the ninth or tenth century in Vienna, one of the tenth or twelfth century in the British Museum, one of the twelfth century in the Vatican (which also has one of the seventeenth century). The Bibliothèque Nationale, Paris, claims four, one each of the eleventh, twelfth, thirteenth, and fourteenth centuries; and there seems to have been one in Copenhagen. Rau (in the book described in the last paragraph of this section of the Introduction) mentions ten MSS. The dates of the MSS suggest that interest in Louis was quite restricted, but nonetheless persistent. Simson, *op cit.,* II, 297, n. 11, cites only one medieval author, Aimoinus, monk of Fleury (d. 1008), who unquestionably made use of the *Vita Hludovici,* although it is true that he used it twice: once in his *Miracula s. Benedicti,* I, 7, and once in his *Vita s. Abbonis,* 20.

The first edition of the *Vita* was the work of the sixteenth-century jurist Pierre Pithou in his *Annalium et historiae Francorum 708–990 scriptores coaetanei XII . . .*

Paris, 1588). Then came two seventeenth-century editions: Marquard Freher included it in *Corpus Francicae historiae veteris et sincerae* . . . (Hannover, 1613); and André Duchesne, in *Historiae Francorum scriptores coaetanei* . . . , II (Paris, 1636). G. C. Joannis incorporated it into his edition of Justus Reuber, *Veterum scriptorum qui Caesarum et imperatorum Germanicorum res per aliquot saecula gestas litteris mandarunt tomus unus* (Frankfurt a/M, 1726); and Martin Bouquet, in *Recueil des historiens des Gaules et de la France*, VI (Paris, 1749). When J. P. Migne published his *Patrologia latina*, he used Duchesne's edition (noted earlier). The best, of course, is the one by G. H. Pertz in MGH (also noted above), but as Manitius has written, "neue dringend nötig!" (but see the last reference in the following paragraph). As of the MSS, one may say of the editions that, however restricted the interest is, it is nonetheless persistent.

The French were apparently the first to translate the *Vita* into a vernacular, a version appearing in vol. III of F. P. G. Guizot, *Collection des memoires relatifs à l'histoire de France* . . . , 31 vols. (Paris, 1823–35). August Potthast, *Wegweiser durch die Geschichtswerke des europäischen Mittelalters bis 1500* (reprint; Graz: Akademische Druck- und Verlagsanstalt, 1954), II, 1376, states that a French version was also available in vol. I of Louis Cousin, *Histoire de l'empire d'Occident* (Paris, 1684), but the table of contents, as given in the *Library of Congress Catalogue of Printed Cards*, mentions only the life of Louis by Thegan. The German translation by Julius von Jasmund (from the MGH edition) first appeared at Leipzig in *Geschichtschreiber der deutschen Vorzeit, 9 Jahrhundert*, ed. G. H. Pertz *et al.*, Band 5 (1850). In 1889 it was reworked by Wilhelm Wattenbach for tome XIX of *Geschichtschreiber* . . . , then reprinted unaltered in 1941. It has been further reworked and reprinted in Reinhold Rau, *Quellen zur Karolingischen Reichsgeschichte*, erster Teil (Berlin: Rütten und Loening, 1956; being Band V of Rudolf Buchner, *Ausgewählte Quellen zur deutschen Geschichte des Mittelalters*), 255–381, together with the Latin text of MGH (critical apparatus omitted) and a short introduction and bibliography. I have found evidence of no other translations.

SOME PRINCIPLES OF THIS TRANSLATION

As the basis of my translation I have used both the MGH and MPL editions, together with a few emendations mentioned in appropriate Notes below. Since I have striven to produce a fair English rendering, I have had to depart on numerous occasions from Latin syntactical constructions. Frequently I have clarified the text by inserting proper names in place of personal pronouns. I have generally given the modern place name where it was available, but I have left in Latin those which have not been identified. Similarly, with few exceptions, I have Anglicized (or at least modernized) names wherever I could. Where the word *Aquae* has occurred I have written *Aix* and where *Aquaegrani* has occurred I have written *Aachen*. The word *placitum* I have invariably rendered as *diet, conventus* as *assembly*, and *concilium* as *council*, so that the reader may know what the Latin word was. I have consistently employed the word *emissary* to translate *missus*, regardless of technicalities. Biblical passages have been translated from the text, but wherever possible I have approximated the language of the Revised Standard Version. Unless otherwise indicated, all translations from other languages are mine.

The division into Parts is my own, although it is fairly

obvious from the text and Part I at least is indicated in the Prologue. Chapter division I have adopted from the edition in MGH. The division into paragraphs is mine and I have taken the liberty of numbering them to facilitate reference. The paragraphs of the Prologue are indicated by numbers enclosed within parentheses, thus Prologue (2), meaning the second paragraph of the Prologue. The particular paragraph of any given chapter is referred to in this manner: Ch. 56:2, meaning the second paragraph of chapter 56.

ACKNOWLEDGMENTS

For specific details, I have recorded my indebtedness to various persons at the appropriate places. Here I have to express gratitude to the Library of Congress and to the libraries of the following universities: Princeton, Saint Louis, Columbia, Cornell, Fordham, Alabama, Chicago, Notre Dame, and Pennsylvania, for the gracious loan of some volumes. To the library of the University of Mississippi and to its Reference Division go my profoundest thanks, for this study was done in its entirety on this campus. To my mother and my sister goes gratitude for innumerable kindnesses in the process of preparing this study.

Several years ago I whimsically dedicated a little book "with filial, fraternal, and avuncular piety to the women in my life: my mother, my sister, and my niece." Now I can add a fourth; so, with "magnavuncular" pride and piety, I inscribe this book to my dear little great-niece, Lisa Ann Orsburn, who can always distract me from concern with circumstances of the ninth century.

The Text

PROLOGUE

(1) When the deeds of the ancients, good or bad, and especially of princes, are reduced to a narrative, a twofold advantage is conferred upon the readers. It serves on one hand to benefit and edify them; on the other, to make them cautious. For since illustrious men stand on high like watch-towers and therefore cannot escape attention, the more their renown is spread abroad, the more widely it is understood. Many people boast that they emulate the more prominent ones as they are intrigued by their goodness. Writers, who by their accounts[1] have striven to teach posterity by what path each prince has trod the way[2] of mortals, report that they treat these memorials of the greater ones for that purpose.[3]

(2) Imitating their zeal we would not be undutiful to those still living or envious of those yet unborn, but we bequeath, albeit in a style less learned, the deeds and life of the orthodox Emperor Louis,[4] a man pleasing to God. I confess without pretence of adulation that the talent of everyone (I do not speak of my own, for it is very modest), even the talent of great writers, withers in the presence of so noble a theme.[5] By divine authority we learn that holy Wisdom teaches sobriety, prudence, justice, and fortitude,

than which nothing in life is sweeter to men.[6] Louis clung
with such constancy to those virtues that one does not know
which he ought the more to admire in him. For what is
soberer than his sobriety, which is designated by another
name, frugality or temperance? He employed it as though
that ancient proverb celebrated to the heavens were quite
familiar to him, "Nothing to excess." [7] He was delighted
by that wisdom which he had learned on the authority of
Scripture, "Behold, the fear of the Lord, that is wisdom." [8]
With what great devotion he cherished justice there are
witnesses who know the zeal with which he burned that
every order of men might render the duties proper to the
rank and that one might love God above all things and his
neighbor as himself.[9] Fortitude, to be sure, had already
enveloped him to such a degree that under God's protection
his unconquerable spirit could be crushed by no hurts although battered by so many notorious ills and although
provoked by wrongs both private and external. To one
fault alone he was by the envious deemed to have succumbed,[10] namely, that he was too mild. But to such persons let us say with the Apostle, "Forgive him this wrong." [11]
Whether these things are true or not, whoever reads this
carefully should be able to discover.

(3) What I have written down to the times of the empire[12] I have learned from the narrative[13] of a most noble
and devout monk, Adhemar[14] who, being of the same age,
was suckled with Louis. Later matters which I witnessed
or which I have been able to ascertain (since I was in the
midst of palace affairs), I have conveyed in my own style.[15]

PART I (CHAPTERS 1–20): A.D. 778–814

Chapter 1. When Charles, most famous of kings,[1] second to none in his own time, undertook sole government of the Frankish kingdom after his father's death[2] and the unfortunate demise of his brother Carloman,[3] he thought that salvation and prosperity would support him invincibly if, in contributing to the peace and concord of the church, he might bind the peaceful ones more closely in brotherly union, discourage the rebellious with impartial severity, and not only take power away from the crushed pagans, but also in some manner lead those enemies of the Christian name to acknowledge and confess the truth. He therefore devoted the inauguration of his reign to these ventures and entrusted to Christ the things to be defended and to be strengthened. After he had with God's approval adjusted affairs in Frankland as he pleased and as he judged suitable, he crossed into Aquitaine, which was always contemplating recurrent wars. Indeed under the leadership of a certain tyrant, Hunold,[4] Aquitaine was even at that moment rushing to arms. But stricken with terror, Hunold was compelled to abandon Aquitaine and save his life by recourse to flight, hiding, and wandering.

2. When this had been accomplished and when public as well as private affairs had been conveniently set in order, he left the most noble and devout Queen Hildigard,[5] pregnant with twins,[6] at a royal villa called Chasseneuil, and crossed the Garonne, the river which is the boundary between Aquitanians and Basques. This district he had long

ago received in a capitulation, when Prince Lupus had surrendered himself and his possessions to Charles's will.[7] When matters there had been completed as opportunity and advantage dictated, he resolved to advance into Spain, if he could overcome the difficulty[8] of the Pyrenees mountains, and with Christ's favor to aid the church which was struggling under the grievous yoke of the Saracens. Although this mountain-range almost reaches heaven by its height, fills one with dread by the roughness of its crags, shrouds one in darkness by the gloom of its forests,[9] it was the narrowness of its passage or rather footpath which almost cut off access not only to the army[10] but also for some time even to a few men. But since Christ was favorable, Charles was able to cross it by a successful march.[11] For the king's courageous purpose (which God ennobled) was to be not inferior to Pompey nor more inactive than Hannibal,[12] who with great harassment to themselves and loss of men and supplies were minded a long time ago to vanquish the difficulty of this place. But, if it is permitted to say so, the treacherous and inconstant alternation of changeable fortune stained the felicity of this crossing. For although those things which could be done in Spain were accomplished and the return march was successfully completed, certain ones in the rear of the royal army met with disaster; they were slaughtered on the same mountain.[13] Since their names have been broadcast far and wide,[14] I have foreborne to declare them.

3. When the king therefore returned, he found that his wife, Hildigard, had given birth to male twins. One of them, snatched away by untimely death, began to die almost before he began to live in the light of day.[15] The other, emerging from his mother's womb with fortunate

result, was reared with the expenses incident to childhood. The twins were born[16] in the seven hundred seventy-eighth year of the Incarnation of our Lord Jesus Christ.[17] When it came to pass that the one who gave promise of vigorous condition was reborn[16] through the sacrament of baptism, it pleased his father for him to be named Louis.[18] To him Charles bequeathed the realm which he had appointed for him when he was born. The wise and sharp-sighted King Charles, knowing further that the realm was like a body, tortured now by this misfortune, now by that, unless its health were sustained and maintained by those physicians, counsel and might,[19] bound the bishops fast to Louis in whatever manner was suitable. Throughout all Aquitaine, moreover, he settled counts, abbots, and many others (whom they popularly call vassals),[20] all of them Franks, whose foresight and might[21] it would not be prudent to hinder with cunning or force. To them as he judged useful he entrusted the care of the kingdom, defense of the frontiers, and supervision of the royal villas. He appointed over the city of Bourges at first Count Humbert, but shortly afterward Count Sturbius; over Poitiers, Abbo; over Périgueux, Widbald; over Auvergne, Iterius; over Wallagiae,[22] Bullus; over Toulouse, Chorso; over Bordeaux, Sigwin; over Albi, Aimo; and over Limoges, Hrodgar.[23]

4:1. When these arrangements had been properly executed, he passed across the Loire with the rest of his forces and retired to Lutetia (which is otherwise called Paris). After a short but discreet lapse of time, a longing gripped him to see Rome, once mistress of the world,[24] to visit the thresholds of the prince of the Apostles[25] and of the teacher of the Gentiles,[26] and to commend himself and his offspring to them. Relying on such advocates (to whom the authority of heaven and earth had been assigned),[27] he would thus be able both to provide for his subjects and to crush the wantonness of treacheries, should they arise. He also reckoned that no modest protection would be bestowed upon him, if both he and his sons could receive from their vicar the royal insignia and a priestly blessing. Since God was favorable, this eventuality came to pass according to his desire. There his son Louis, still wearing the habiliments of the cradle, was marked by the hands of the venerable pontiff Hadrian[28] with the benediction appropriate to one destined to reign and was invested with a royal diadem [781]. When therefore all those things which seemed needful to be done in Rome were performed, King Charles with his sons and his army returned in peace to Frankland. He dispatched his son Louis to Aquitaine to reign as king, sending Arnold[29] with him as escort, and in an orderly and fitting manner[30] constituting others as ministers suitable for the boy's guardianship. Louis was brought to the city of Orléans in the accouterments of the cradle, but there he was girded with arms befitting his age, placed on a horse, and thus with God's favor transported to Aquitaine.

4:2. While Louis remained there a few years, that is, four, the glorious King Charles was waging unremitting and costly campaigns against the Saxons. In the midst of them, however, on guard lest the people of Aquitaine become insolent because of his prolonged absence or lest his son learn strange customs in his tenderer years (from which age once infected is extricated with difficulty),[31] he sent a full military escort to bring his son, a good rider, to him. Marquises were left behind to protect the frontiers of the kingdom and to ward off enemy incursions if by chance they should attack. His son, readily obeying in order to

learn how to rule, met Charles at Paderborn. Louis was
clothed in the habit of the Basque boys of his own age, with
the round mantle, the sleeves of the shirt long and flowing, full trousers, spurs attached to the little boots,[32] and
a dart in his hand, for his father had ordered these things.
The son remained beside his father, going thence with him
to Eresburg, until the sun declined from its high point and
allayed the summer heat with autumnal mildness. Receiving
permission from his father at the end of that period, he
returned to winter in Aquitaine.

5. At that season Chorso,[33] duke of Toulouse, was ambushed, bound by bonds of oaths, and then released by
the guile of a certain Basque named Adelericus. To avenge
this blot, King Louis and the magnates by whose advice
the commonwealth of Aquitaine was administered appointed a general assembly at a place in Septimania called
Mors-Gothorum.[34] The Basque was summoned, yet aware
of his deed refused to appear until exchange of hostages.
But allowing nothing to imperil the hostages and having
been given favors, he restored ours, received his own, and
so withdrew. During the following summer [790], by command of his father, King Louis came to Worms for a
simple visit, not for an expedition. He stayed with him
during the winter. There Adelericus, ordered to present
his case before the king and having been heard, wishing to
answer the charges, but not being able, was outlawed and
banished in irrevocable exile. Chorso (by whose negligence
such disgrace had happened to the king and to the Franks)
was removed from the dukedom of Toulouse, and William[35]
was substituted for him. The latter found the Basques (by
nature capricious) excited because of the aforesaid event
and enraged because of Adelericus's punishment. In a short

time he subdued them by speech as well as by force and imposed peace upon the nation. In the same year King Louis held a general diet at Toulouse.[36] While it was in session Abutaurus,[37] duke of the Saracens, and others bordering on the kingdom of Aquitaine dispatched messengers to him seeking peace and sending royal gifts. Received according to the king's favor, the messengers then returned to their own lands.

6:1. Meanwhile, in the following year, King Louis met the king his father at Ingelheim and from there went with him to Regensburg. Having reached the years of adolescence, he was there girded with the sword.[38] After having accompanied his father (who was leading an army against the Avars) as far as Chuneberg, he was ordered to go back and remain with Queen Fastrada[39] until his father's return. He therefore spent the approaching winter with her, while his father continued the expedition which he had undertaken. But when the latter was returning from the Avar campaign [792], Louis received from him a command to go back to Aquitaine and from there to advance to Italy with as great an army as possible to aid his brother Pepin.[40] Obediently he went back to Aquitaine in the autumn. Everything relating to the defense of the realm having been set in order, he rode through the harsh and tortuous windings of Mont Cenis[41] down into Italy, and celebrating the Lord's Nativity [793] in Ravenna, he came to his brother. Combining their forces, they entered the province of Beneventum together, ravaged all the enemy territory, and took possession of a fortress. When the winter had passed, they returned together successfully to their father.

6:2. A report, however, darkened their great haste: they learned that their natural brother Pepin[42] had planned a

rebellion against their common father, and that as a result
many of the nobles who had espoused this crime had been
trapped and destroyed. Advancing swiftly to Bavaria, they
came to their father at the place called Salz, where they
were agreeably received by him. King Louis spent what
remained of summer and the autumn and winter with the
king his father. For the latter was exceedingly careful that
no honorable nurture should escape the king his son, or
that outward matters should in any way disgrace him. In
early spring, when Louis was being sent away by his father,
Charles asked him why, since he was a king, he was of such
severe plainness in household matters that he would never
offer himself a benefit unless requested to do so. Charles
learned from Louis that a lord in name only may be treated
as in want of everything, since all of the nobles, so careful
of private matters, are with perverse course neglectful of
public affairs, and public lands are thereby turned into
private properties. To obviate such dire need, but keenly
desirous that affection for his son among the magnates
suffer no diminution, if Louis himself should discreetly recover something which he had once transferred to them
through inexperience, Charles sent his own emissaries,
Wilbert,[43] afterwards archbishop of the see of Rouen, and
Count Richard,[44] overseer of his villas, decreeing that the
villas which had hitherto served for royal use be restored
to public service. That was accordingly done.

7. When these matters had been undertaken, the king
showed proof of his foresight and disclosed the disposition
of his mercy.[45] He ordained that he would establish winter
quarters in four places, namely, the palaces at Doué, Chasseneuil, Angeac, and Ebreuil, so that after a lapse of three
years each place would support him during the winter in

the fourth year only. Those places would then offer sufficient provision for the royal household when it came back
for the fourth year. With these things very wisely arranged,
Louis forbade that military provender (which they popularly call "fodder")[46] be furnished any more by the common folk. Although the military personnel bore this reluctantly, that man of mercy, considering both the penury
of those who did the furnishings and the harshness of those
who compel them, as well as the desperation of both,
deemed it preferable to supply his men from his own stores,
rather than by allowing them to forage and run into
dangers. At that time he relieved by his liberality the
people of Albi of the tribute of wine and grain with which
they were burdened. He had with him Meginharius,[47] a
wise and vigorous man, skilled in the royal advantage and
honor, sent to him by his father. These arrangements are
said to have pleased his father so much that in imitation he
in turn forbade military provisions to be given as tribute
in Frankland. Rejoicing in the happy progress of his son,
Charles moreover enjoined that many other things be cor-
rected.

8. In the following season the king came to Toulouse and
there held a general assembly [795]. He received, then dismissed in peace, the emissaries whom Alfonso,[48] prince of
Galicia, had sent with gifts to strengthen friendship. Louis
also received and dismissed the emissaries of Bahaluc [Bahlul
ben Machluk], duke of the Saracens (whose princedom was
in the mountainous regions next to Aquitaine), who had
come seeking peace and bringing gifts.[49] At that time fearing that he might be dragged into the manifold toils of lust
by the natural heat of the body,[50] Louis betrothed Irmingard [51] with the advice of his men. The future queen was

born of illustrious lineage,[52] the daughter of Count Ingram-
nus. He also decreed a very strong defense along all the
frontiers of Aquitaine. He fortified and colonized the city
of Vich, the fortress of Cardona, Casseres, and other cities
formerly deserted, entrusting them to Count Burrellus[53] to
be guarded with suitable troops.

9. When winter had passed, the king his father sent Louis
a message to come with whatever people he could muster
and move with him against the Saxons. Without delay he
came to him at Aachen and with him proceeded to Frie-
mersheim on the banks of the Rhine where Charles held a
general diet [799]. Louis remained in Saxony with his
father until Martinmas.[54] Afterwards he left Saxony and
withdrew to Aquitaine, a great part of the winter having
been spent with his father.

10. In the succeeding summer King Charles sent him a
command to accompany him to Italy, but the plan was
altered and he was ordered to remain at home. Charles,
however, proceeded to Rome and there received the imperial fillets,[55] while King Louis went away again to Toulouse and thence marched into Spain. As he was approaching
Barcelona, Zaddo,[56] duke of the city, met him as a subject,
but did not surrender the city. Bypassing it, therefore, and
pressing upon Lérida, the king subjugated and overthrew it.
After the destruction of Lérida and after other towns had
been laid waste and burned, he marched on Huesca. A band
of soldiers cut, devastated, and burned the fields full of
crops; and whatever was found outside the city was consumed by a ruinous conflagration. With those activities completed, he returned to his own lands, since winter was already at hand.

11. Later, when summer was burgeoning [804], the most

glorious Emperor Charles repaired to Saxony, commanding his son to follow him, ready to winter in that land. In haste Louis came to Neuss, there crossed the Rhine, and sped to meet his father. But before he reached him, he encountered a messenger from his father at a place named Ostfaloa[57] with orders to weary himself no longer in traveling, but rather to pitch camp in an advantageous position and there await his return. For the entire Saxon nation had been conquered and Emperor Charles was already on his way back as victor. When his son met him, Charles kissed him in a prolonged embrace, extolled him with gratitude and praise, and proclaimed the value of his prompt obedience, repeating again and again that he was fortunate in such a son. Since the long and exceedingly bloody Saxon war, which, as they say, filled an interval of thirty-three years,[58] had at length come to an end, King Louis, dismissed by his father, gathered his followers and returned to his own kingdom for the winter.

12. The winter having passed, Emperor Charles, now at an opportune season [800] and at rest from foreign wars, began to visit the places of his realm bordering on the sea. When King Louis learned about that, sending Adhemar[59] as legate to Rouen, he besought his father to turn aside into Aquitaine and renew acquaintance with the kingdom which he had granted to Louis by coming to the place called Chasseneuil. His father received the invitation honorably and thanked his son, yet denied the request and ordered him to appear at Tours. Coming thither the son, joyfully received by his father, accompanied him to Ver as he was returning to Frankland. Departing thence he made his way back to Aquitaine.

13:1. In the following summer Zaddo, duke of Barcelona,

was persuaded by a certain friend (as he thought) to advance to Narbonne, but was captured and brought first to King Louis, then to Charles his father. At that very time King Louis was holding deliberations about things which should be done, the people of his realm having been gathered together at Toulouse. For when Burgundio died, his county of Fezensac was assigned to Liutard.[60] At that action the Basques took offense and burst into so great a wantonness that they slew some of Liutard's men with the sword, burned others with fire. When they were summoned, they at first refused to come. Later, however, they came to plead their cause, but they suffered the penalties due for such daring deeds,[61] certain ones being committed to the flames by the *lex talionis*.

13:2. These transactions having been accomplished, in the season following it appeared to the king and his counselors that they ought to go and besiege Barcelona. When the army was thereupon divided into three parts,[62] Louis retained one with himself while he tarried at Rousillon; he enjoined upon another (which Count Rotstagnus of Gerona commanded) the investiture of the city; but the third he dispatched to take up a position beyond the city so that those besieging it might not be unexpectedly surrounded. Meanwhile those shut up within the city sent to Córdoba and demanded assistance. The king of the Saracens immediately dispatched an army to aid them. While they who had been sent were approaching Saragossa, information was relayed about the army appointed to meet them along the way. Furthermore, William was there first, as also the standard-bearer Adhemar,[63] and with them a strong force. Hearing that, the Saracens turned aside against the Asturians and without warning inflicted slaughter upon them, but

they reported it as much more serious than it was. While the
Saracens were withdrawing, our men returned to their
comrades who were besieging the city and together with
them they completely encompassed it. Permitting no one
to enter or leave it, they disquieted it until the inhabitants
were compelled by bitterness of famine to pluck the oldest
skins from the doors[64] and turn them into an unfruitful
food. Others, preferring death to an unhappy life, hurled
themselves from the parapets. Still others were animated by
a vain hope[65] that the Franks would be stayed from the
siege by the severity of winter. But the counsel of prudent
men cut off that hope. For timber was brought up from all
sides and they began to construct barracks as though to
remain there during the winter. The citizens then lost hope
and, turning to final desperation, betrayed their prince, a
kinsman of Zaddo named Hamur, whom they had appointed
in place of Zaddo.[66] In the following manner they surrendered themselves and the city after the besiegers had
granted them an opportunity to withdraw.

13:3. Our men understood that the city was wearied by
the long siege and they believed that it would presently be
captured or delivered up. By a fitting and honorable decision, therefore, they invited the king so that a city of
such fair fame might extend the royal prestige with glory
if it should happen to capitulate with him present. King
Louis readily assented to this honorable suggestion. He
came immediately to his army entrenched about the city
which had endured continuous assault for six weeks, but
which, now vanquished, submitted to the victor. The city
was thereupon surrendered and thrown open. On the first
day the king ordered guards for it, but he himself refrained
from entering until he might determine how to dedicate to

God's glory with suitable thanksgiving the coveted and successful victory. On the morrow, then, with priests and clergy going before him and his army, he entered the gate of the city with solemn splendor and hymns of praise and proceeded to the church of the holy and most victorious Cross to give thanks to God for the victory divinely bestowed upon him. Leaving Count Bera[67] there with forces of Goths as guard, Louis returned to his own lands[68] to spend the winter. Discovering the dangerous threat against him from the Saracens, his father had sent Louis's brother Charles[69] to provide assistance. As Charles, however, was passing Lyons and hastening to the aid of his brother, a messenger of the king his brother announced that the city had been taken and advised him to weary himself no further. Thereupon, returning from that place, Charles went back to his father.

14:1. While King Louis was spending the winter in Aquitaine, the king his father[70] requested his presence at a conference in Aachen on the Purification of Holy Mary Mother of God.[71] Appearing before him, he remained with him as long as seemed good, but left during the Lenten season.[72] The succeeding summer he set out for Spain with as large a warlike panoply as had ever been seen.[73] Marching through Barcelona and coming to Tarragona, he seized those whom he found there, causing others to flee. His military force razed all installations, fortresses, and towns as far as Tortosa, a ravaging fire being the instrument of destruction. Meanwhile at a place named Santa Coloma he divided his troops into two parts, taking as large a portion as possible with himself against Tortosa. Then he expeditiously steered Isembard, Adhemar, Bera, Burrellus,[74] with the remainder, to the upper places, so that crossing the Ebro they might attack the enemy unexpectedly from ambush while the foes were lingering safely in their residences. Failing that, they might at least throw the region into a state of disorder and the inhabitants into a state of alarm. While the king, therefore, was pushing toward Tortosa, the others, moving during the nights to the upper courses of the Ebro, seeking during the days the shelter of forests, marched until they crossed both the Cinca and the Ebro by swimming. Spending six days on this journey, they crossed on the seventh. As soon as all had come out of the water unharmed, they laid waste the land of the enemy far and wide, and penetrated even to their greatest villa, which is called Villa Rubea.[75] From it they took great spoil since the enemy were unprepared, not expecting any such eventuality.

14:2. When these things had been accomplished, those who had been able to escape the blow proclaimed it through the length and breadth of the land. As a result large bands of Saracens and Moors were assembled and ready to meet them at the mouth of the valley which is called Vallis Ibana.[76] The nature of the valley is such that it lies in an abyss, surrounded on this side and that by high, precipitous mountains.[77] If God's providence had not prevented our men from entering, they would have perished from the blows of the stones almost without effort on the part of the foe, or they would have fallen into the hands of the enemy. But while the latter were blocking the way, our men are seeking a more open and level area in another direction. The Moors, supposing that our men were doing this not so much for the sake of protection but rather out of fear, follow them along the ridge. Our men, however, left booty behind, bared their face to the foe, made a stand, and with Christ's aid compelled the Moors to turn their backs. They seized many, slew them, then returned cheerfully to the booty which they had left. Finally, after twenty days of digression, they went back in haste to the king, only a few of them having been lost. King Louis received them gladly and returned home since the enemy territory was everywhere devastated.

15:1. In the following year [810] King Louis again made ready a campaign into Spain. His father prevented him from proceeding thither in person. For Charles had given orders for ships to be constructed[78] at that season in all the rivers which flowed into the sea[79] to serve against the inroads of the Northmen. He enjoined this duty upon his son in respect of the Rhone, Garonne, and Silida.[80] But he sent his own emissary, Ingobert, to represent his son in Spain and in place of them both to lead the army against the foe. While the king was continuing in Aquitaine for the aforesaid reason, his army reached Barcelona by a fortunate march. There, taking counsel among themselves how they could come upon the enemy by a secret attack, they devised this plan. Building boats to carry them across the Ebro, they divided each of them into four parts, since a fourth part of each boat could be transported overland by two horses or mules. With cudgels and hammers the boats could be readily fitted together again, and with pitch, wax, and tow the seams of the structures could be closed up as soon as they were brought to the river. When they had been built, the larger part of the army sought Tortosa with the aforesaid emissary Ingobert. But those who had been appointed to the boat-building, that is Adhemar,[81] Bera, and the rest—a journey of three days being anticipated (for they were without pack-saddles)—were at length on the fourth day transported across the Ebro in the reassembled boats.

They had used the sky for a covering, abjured fire lest they be betrayed by the smoke, concealed themselves in the forests in the daytime, and traveled as far as possible by night.[82] The horses they entrusted to swimming.

15:2. This marvelous feat had given effect to their desire, otherwise it would have been violently overthrown. For when Abaidun, duke of Tortosa, was blockading the banks of the Ebro river, and those of whom we have spoken above were crossing its upper courses in the foregoing manner, a certain Moor entered the river to bathe and saw horse-dung floating downstream. Observing it (they are extremely shrewd), swimming to seize the dung, and applying it to his nostrils, he cried out, "Look, companions, I warn you, beware! This excrement is not that of a wild ass or of any animal accustomed to grassy fodder. On my word, I am certain that these are horse-droppings; I am certain that these have once been barley and hence the food of horses or mules. Watch therefore very carefully, for in the upper courses of this river, I believe, an ambush is being laid for us." Immediately they directed two of their men to mount horses and explore. Descrying our men, they brought word to Abaidun that the report was true. Yet compelled by fear to abandon everything in camp as unimportant, they took to flight. Our men, having captured everything left behind, entertained themselves that night in the pavilions of the Saracens. But assembling a great band of the enemy, Abaidun went out on the morrow to meet our men and give them battle. Ours by trusting in divine help, although weaker and much less numerous, put their foes to flight and filled the road with slaughter of those fleeing. And indeed ours did not restrain their hands from carnage until the light of the sun and of the day declined, the shades of night overspread the land, and the light of the stars mounted to relieve the night. When these things had been done, by Christ's favor, they rejoined their own men with high glee and with prizes. After a while they marched back homeward leaving the city invested.

16. In the very next year King Louis decided to revisit Tortosa in person, taking with him Heribert,[83] Liutard, Isembard, and a strong force from Frankland. Arriving there he battered it with rams, mangonels, sheds, and other engines to such a degree that its citizens lost all hope[84] and, perceiving that their own men were exhausted by unfortunate war,[85] surrendered the keys of the city. These he carried to his father and returned in high favor. This affair struck mighty terror in the Saracens and Moors, for they feared that an equal fate might befall each city. After forty days of indecisive siege, the king came back from Tortosa and entered his own realm.

17:1. But when the current year [812] was over, he set an army in order and decided to send it against Huesca with Heribert,[86] his father's emissary. Those who had been dispatched arrived there and laid siege to the city. Anyone who opposed them they either captured or drove into flight. But while in position around the city and relaxing more slothfully than was fitting, some imprudent and capricious youths approached the walls[87] and attempted first to harass with words those who manned the ramparts, then to assault them with missiles.[88] The townsmen, thereupon, despising the small number of besiegers and anticipating a late arrival of reinforcements, opened the gates and made a sally. A battle took place: the slain fell on both sides, but finally the enemy withdrew into the city and the others returned to camp to wait.

17:2. Prolonging the siege therefore, devastating on a large scale, and satisfying as much as possible their wrath against the foes, our men returned to the king who was at that time in the forests eagerly absorbed in hunting (for it was at the very end of autumn). After he had received the men returning from the expedition on which he had dispatched them earlier, the king spent the ensuing winter in peace, staying on his own lands.

18:1. When summer came, however, a general assembly of his people having been summoned, he informed them of a rumor which had reached him, namely, that a certain portion of the Basques, who had some time ago been received in surrender, were now resolved upon revolt and were rising in rebellion. The public welfare demanded for him to go and repress their stubbornness.[89] Everyone applauded[90] the king's desire and declared that such things should not be permitted among the conquered, but should rather be severely restrained. The army therefore having been mobilized and set in order as was proper, he came to the villa of Dax and gave command that those who were being charged with disloyalty come to him. When they refused to appear, he went down to their neighborhood and allowed all their properties to be plundered by a band of soldiers. At last, when everything known to belong to them had been destroyed, they came as suppliants. In the end they earned pardon instead of punishment, since all their possessions had already been lost.

18:2. Thereafter, having crossed the difficult passage of the Pyrenean Alps, he descended upon Pamplona; and delaying in those places as long as seemed appropriate, he settled matters which might be advantageous for both public and private welfare. When it became needful to go back through the narrow fastnesses of that mountain, the Basques attempted their native and accustomed habit of craft, but they were themselves ensnared by a shrewd, cunning plan which enabled our men to evade them safely and cautiously. For one of them who had gone forward to give challenge was captured and hanged; then wives or sons were seized as hostages from almost all the rest and held until our men could reach a place where Basque artifice would not be able to inflict damage upon the king or the army.

19:1. These things accomplished, the king and his people departed to his lands, God being favorable. From the very beginning of his life,[91] but especially at that time, the most pious mind of the king was intent on the worship of God and exaltation of holy church. His works indeed cried out not only that he was a king, but even more that he was a priest. In all Aquitaine before it was entrusted to him, he who appeared to be a clergyman, a functionary under tyrants, had known how to give attention more to riding, warlike exercise, and the hurling of missiles than to divine worship. But by the king's zeal teachers were brought in from everywhere, the study of reading, singing, and understanding of divine and humane letters[92] increased more quickly than one would have believed. It was especially owing to the influence of those abandoning all their possessions for the love of God, who were minded to become partners in the speculative life. Before Aquitaine came under his governance, this order [monasticism] had fallen into ruins; under him it regained its vigor to such a degree that he himself also, desiring eagerly to emulate the memorable example of his grandfather's brother Carloman, aspired to embrace the pinnacles of the contemplative life. His father's resistance provided an obstacle that he might not

become a partaker of that vow, or rather it was the pleasure
of divine will which did not want a man of such eminent
piety to hide away in anxiety for his own salvation alone, but
through him and under him for the salvation of many to
flourish. Many monasteries were repaired by him in the
exercise of his sovereignty, many erected from the founda-
tions, notably the following:[93] the monasteries of Saint
Filibert, Saint Florent, Charroux, Conques, Saint Maixent,
Menate, Maulieu, Moissac, Saint Savin, Massay, Nouaillé,
Saint Theotfrid, Saint Pascentius, Dousère, and Solignac,
the female cloisters of Saint Mary[94] and Saint Radegunda,[95]
the monasteries of Devera, Deutera in the Toulousain, Vadala, in Septimania Aniane, Gellone, Saint Lawrence, Saint
Mary (called "in Rubine" or "in Orubione"),[96] Caunes, and
many, many others with which the whole realm of Aquitaine
is adorned as with lamps.

19:2. Imitating his example, not only many bishops, but
also a great many laymen, restored monasteries which had
fallen into ruins and vied in establishing new ones, a fact
which is for the eyes of all to see. At last the commonwealth of the Aquitanian realm had progressed into such
felicity that, whether it pleased the king to travel or to
remain at his palace, hardly anyone might be found complaining justly that he had suffered anything. Three days
every week the king was available for judicial proceedings.[97]
Once Archambald,[98] imperial notary, entrusted by Charles
with certain matters of state to be laid before Louis for his
advice, on returning to his master explained this regulation
as he had observed it. Charles is reputed to have boasted
to such a degree that he burst into tears with unwonted
readiness, saying to those standing about, "Let us rejoice, O
my companions, that we have been vanquished by the

mature wisdom of this youth!" Since Louis was a faithful
servant of the Lord in what was confided to him, farseeing
in augmenting the talent given to him, he was appointed as
one having authority in the entire household of his father.[99]

20:1. Since Pepin, King of Italy, had been dead for some
time,[100] and since his brother Charles had even more recently
abandoned human affairs in the same way,[101] the hope of
a world to be possessed swelled up in Louis.[102] For while
Gerricus, the falconer,[103] sent to discuss certain needs with
Louis's father, was lingering in the palace awaiting a reply
to his reports, he was admonished by Franks as well as by
Germans that the king should come to his father and be
present near him. They stated that since his father seemed
already to be sinking into old age[104] and was enduring with
bitterness the unhappy passing of his children, these things
portended his speedy bodily dissolution. When Gerricus
related this to the king and the king in turn to his advisers,
the proposal seemed a wholesome one to some of them, or
rather to virtually all of them. But with profounder counsel
the king delayed in so doing lest by such action he render
himself an object of his father's suspicion. Notwithstanding
these things, Deity, for fear and love of Whom Louis did
not wish to do that, disposed more providentially, since it
is His wont in respect of those who love Him to ennoble
them more sublimely than one can imagine.[105] For thereafter the king was cheerfully indulgent to those seeking
peace whom he had been accustomed to weary with warfare,
and an armistice of two years was maintained.

20:2. In the meanwhile Emperor Charles, realizing that
he was rapidly ebbing into the depths of old age, and
fearing that when he had been withdrawn from human
affairs the kingdom would be left bewildered which by

God's gift had been so nobly ruled, sent and summoned his
son from Aquitaine lest it be plagued by tumults without
or disquieted by schisms within. He received Louis courte-
ously and kept him with him during the entire summer,
instructing him about those things which were deemed needful. He advised him how the kingdom should be nurtured,
governed, and arranged, and how what had been arranged
should be maintained. Finally he crowned him with the
imperial diadem[106] and informed him that with Christ's
favor supreme power would be his. Thereafter he gave him
leave to return to his own lands. Departing from his father
in the month of November, Louis revisited Aquitaine.

20:3. His father, near death, began to suffer depression
with frequent and strange inconveniences. By such tokens,
of course, as though by certain messengers, death was
announcing that its coming would be very soon. At length,
therefore, defects of the biles struggling against each other
and attacking his strength, the weakness of nature gave
way and Charles took to his bed. Daily and hourly nearer
to death, he finished his last day[107] just as he caused his
possessions to be divided by law. An almost ineluctable
grief was left to the kingdom of the Franks.[108] Yet in his
successor Scripture was proven truthful, which in such
events says to comfort the minds of those who mourn,
"Dead is the righteous man, but as though he is not dead,
for he has left an heir, a son like himself." [109] On the fifth
day before the Kalends of February[110] died the most pious
Emperor Charles, in the year of the Incarnation of our
Lord Jesus Christ the eight hundred fourteenth.[111] At that
time, as though by some premonition, Emperor Louis had
publicly announced to the people a general council for
the Purification of Holy Mary Mother of God[112] in the
place named Doué.

Chapter 21.1. When Charles of holy memory had died, Rampo[1] was sent to Louis by the attendants at the funeral, by the children[2] and magnates of the palace, that he might be informed of the death and that he might in no way delay his coming. As Louis was approaching the city of Orléans, Theodulf, bishop of the see and very learned in all matters,[3] was apprised beforehand. Hurriedly dispatching a reporter to the emperor, Theodulf was eager to discover whether to stand ready as Louis entered the city or to meet him by some route before he entered. Upon consideration Louis discerned the reason[4] and forthwith commanded him to come out to him. Thereafter Louis received sorrowful messengers one after another. After the fifth day he directed his steps from that place and hastened his journey with as many people as perplexity of the time allowed. For Wala,[5] possessor of the highest rank with Emperor Charles,[6] was greatly feared: it was thought that he might plot something sinister against the new emperor. Wala nevertheless came to Louis with all speed and, according to the custom of the Franks, submitted with humble acquiescence, commending himself to the new emperor's will. When he had come to do homage, other Frankish magnates vied in imitation, earnestly and in droves, to meet Louis. Finally he reached Heristal with a favorable journey, and on the thirteenth day after he had removed from Aquitaine[7] he happily placed his foot in the palace of Aachen.[8]

21:2. Although by nature very mild he had made up his

mind long ago about the activities of his sisters in his father's dwelling[9] (by which blemish alone his father's house was being undermined). Wishing to be rid of that inconvenience and at the same time being on guard lest what had once happened through Odilo and Hiltrud[10] revive a scandal, he sent for Wala and Warnarius as well as for Lantbert and Ingobert.[11] At Aachen they were to look cautiously into such things lest more should happen and also to observe carefully certain ones who by excessive debauchery and arrogant pride were guilty of *lèse-majesté* at the emperor's entrance. For although some of them had asked for pardon as suppliants while his journey was in progress, they were nonetheless guilty. At the same time he hoped that people who did not come out to meet him might await his arrival there without fear. But without the knowledge of Wala, Ingobert, and Louis's nephew Lantbert, just appointed, Count Warnarius ordered Hodoin, who was already liable to the crime mentioned, to be arrested and exposed to the royal judgment. The latter, forewarned, suspected a plot, for remorse was stinging bitterly. Because he refused to obey, although deserving to be tried, he brought destruction upon Warnarius. For coming as Warnarius had commanded, he killed him and made Lantbert a cripple for a long time with an injury of the leg. He himself, however, was pierced by a sword and slain. When these things had been announced to the emperor, the death of his friend dissuaded his mind from mercy to such a degree that a certain Tullius,[12] who seemed almost worthy of the king's pardon or clemency, was punished by loss of his eyes.

22. Coming then to the palace of Aix, the emperor was received with great applause by his relatives and many

thousands of Franks, and was for the second time proclaimed emperor. Having disposed of these matters, he expressed thanks to those who had been thoughtful of his father's burial and brought the solace of appropriate condolence to kinsmen consumed with bitter grief. What was lacking in the funeral obsequies of his father, he quickly supplied. When his father's will had been read, nothing remained of his father's goods to be distributed according to Louis's discretion, for nothing had been left intestate. What Charles had thought should be apportioned to the metropolitan churches, he had divided by indicating the names, of which there were twenty-one. What was fit for royal equipment[13] he had left to a later time. He had also decreed what should, according to Christian custom, be bequeathed to sons and sons' sons and daughters, to royal servants both male and female, and to the poor folk in common. As Lord Louis the emperor read what was written, he fulfilled all those things, dutifully performing the task.[14]

23:1. When these affairs had been completed, the emperor gave sentence that the entire female company (which was very large) be excluded from the palace, except the very few whom he considered fit for the royal service. Each of his sisters withdrew to her own lands which she had received from her father. Although they did not deserve of the emperor such treatment as they got, they yielded to his commands.

23:2. Afterwards, respecting the embassies destined for his father but coming to him, the emperor received them with earnestness and listened to them. He tendered them banquets, then sent them away dowered with expensive gifts. Of them the chief one was from the Emperor Michael of Constantinople,[15] to whom Lord Charles had dispatched as his emissaries Amalarius, bishop of Trèves, and Peter,[16] abbot of Nonantola, to confirm peace. On their return they brought with them emissaries from the aforesaid Michael, Christopher the first swordsman, and Gregory, a deacon, who were accredited to Charles to make reply about all the things which had been written. When the emperor dismissed them, he sent with them his own emissaries[17] to Leo, Michael's successor,[18] Nortbert,[19] bishop of Reggio, and Richoin,[20] count of Poitiers, desiring an alliance and a renewal of old friendship and also a confirmation of the agreement.[21]

23:3. In the same year he held a general assembly at Aachen. Throughout all parts of his realm he sent loyal and trusted men,[22] firmly attached to just law and clothed with his authority, to correct evil things and to mete out fitting justice to all with equal balance. Bernard,[23] his nephew and for a long time king of Italy, summoned to his presence and obediently complying, Louis allowed to go back to his own kingdom dowered with ample gifts.[24] Grimoald, prince of the Beneventans, did not come in person but sent his ambassadors. Him he constrained by contract and oaths to contribute every year to the public treasury seven thousand *solidi* of gold.

24:1. In the same year he sent his two sons Lothair and Pepin to Bavaria and Aquitaine respectively, but the third, Louis, still in the years of boyhood, he kept with him.[25] At the same time also Heriold,[26] to whom the entire kingdom of the Danes was supposed to belong[27] and who had been driven from that kingdom by the sons of Godefrid,[28] took asylum with Emperor Louis and according to the custom of the Franks entrusted himself to his hands. Having received him, the king ordered him to go to Saxony and there conceal himself for a time until he could bring him help to recover his princedom.

24:2. At that time imperial clemency restored to the Saxons and Frisians their ancestral heritage, which because of treachery they had legally lost under his father. Some attributed this act to generosity, others to lack of foresight, on the grounds that since these people were accustomed to native savagery, they ought to be bridled with such reins that they could not dash unrestrained into shameless[29] treason. The emperor, however, supposing that they would be bound to him the more closely to the degree in which he showered kindness upon them, was not deceived in his hope. For afterwards he held the same people as always most devoted to him.

25:1. When this year completed its course, it was reported to the emperor that some powerful Romans had entered into a vicious conspiracy against Leo the Apostolic.[30] The apostolic man had adjudged them to be taken away and tried by deadly torture,[31] the law of the Romans being in harmony with that. When the emperor heard these things he was reluctant to believe that punishment had been imposed so severely by the chief priest of the world. He therefore sent King Bernard of Italy thither to investigate what truth or falsity rumor had spread in this matter and to report to him through Gerold.[32] King Bernard then entered Rome and through the aforesaid emissary reported what had been observed. But soon followed the emissaries of Leo the Apostolic, Bishop John[33] of Selva Candida, Theodore[34] the *nomenclator*, and Duke Sergius. They excused Leo the Apostolic for the alleged offenses.

25:2. Thereafter the emperor ordered the Saxon and Obotrite counts, formerly subject to Lord Charles, to give aid

to Heriold in reclaiming his own realm, Baldricus[35] being
sent as legate for this purpose. When these counts had
crossed the river Eider, they came down into the land of
the Northmen to the place called Sinlendi.[36] Although the
sons of Godefrid were abundantly supplied with troops and
two hundred ships, they did not want to approach and
engage in battle.[37] There was consequently a mutual withdrawal, everything which the counts could destroy being
set afire and forty hostages being taken by them. With this
achievement they returned to the emperor at a place called
Paderborn, where all the people had gathered for a general
assembly.

25:3. To Paderborn also came all the princes and nobles
of the eastern Slavs. Abulat,[38] king of the Saracens, sought
from the emperor a three-year truce, which was at first
granted but later rejected as worthless. War with the
Saracens was thereupon resumed. Bishop Nortbert and
Count Richoin came back from Constantinople and brought
favorable proposals of treaty between the Greeks and the
Franks. At the same season, when Leo the Apostolic was
already burdened with adversities, the Romans attempted to
steal all the farms which they call "estates" [39] and which had
been recently established by the apostolic man, as well as
those things which they alleged were robbed of them
contrary to law, since no judge had rendered decision.
Through Winigis, duke of Spoleto, King Bernard withstood
their undertaking and dispatched to the emperor a courier
who knew about these events.

26:1. After the emperor had passed the harsh winter in
sound health and peaceful success and when the favorable
mildness of summertime [816] was coming on, those who
are called eastern Franks and the counts of the Saxon na-

tion were dispatched by him against the Slavic Sorbs who
were reported to have revolted against his domination.
Christ granting it, the efforts of these Slavs were suppressed
very quickly and easily. But the nearest of the Basques, who
dwell in places close to the ridge of the Pyrenees, deserted
us at the same time in accordance with their innate fickle-
ness. The cause of the rebellion was the emperor's removal
of their Count Sigiwin from chieftaincy over them. The
purpose of that action had been to chastise their perverse
behavior which he deemed almost intolerable. They were
tamed to such a degree by two campaigns that too late
they repented of their endeavors and with great eagerness
sought to capitulate.

26:2. In the midst of these events the falling asleep of
Lord Leo, bishop of Rome, which occurred on the eighth
day before the Kalends of June[40] in the twenty-first year
of his episcopate, was announced to the emperor, as well
as the accession of the deacon Stephen[41] to his position. The
latter lost no time in coming to the Lord Emperor after
his consecration. For two months had scarcely elapsed before he hurried with urgent speed to meet Louis. He sent
ahead an embassy to satisfy the emperor about his succession. Anticipating his approach, the emperor ordered his
nephew Bernard to accompany him. He also directed others
to be sent to conduct him with due honor as he drew nearer.
Louis decided to receive his arrival at Rheims and ordered
Hildebald, archchaplain of the sacred palace, Theodulf,
bishop of Orléans, John of Arles,[42] and a host of other
ministers of the church, clad in priestly fillets, to meet him.
Lastly the emperor walked in state from the thousand-monk
cloister of the holy confessor Remigius and received the
vicar of blessed Peter in a most honorable manner; he as-

sisted him in dismounting from his horse and supported him with his own hand as he was entering the church, various ecclesiastical ranks marching in front singing *Te Deum laudamus*. This hymn finished, the clergy of Rome acclaimed the emperor with the due *Laudes*,[43] which the Apostolic Lord completed with a collect.

26:3. Afterwards there was a session within the sanctuary of the house. When the reasons for his coming had been rehearsed and the consecrated bread and wine had been shared, the Apostolic Lord remained there while the emperor returned to the city. On the morrow the Lord Emperor called upon the Apostolic Lord, tendered him a sumptuous banquet, and honored him with extensive gifts. In like manner, on the third day, the Lord Emperor was invited by the Apostolic Lord and was dowered with many different favors. On the next day, which was the Lord's Day,[44] the emperor was crowned with the imperial diadem and signed with a blessing amid the festivities of Mass. All these things at length completed, the Apostolic Lord returned to Rome, having obtained everything that he had asked. The emperor then retired to Compiègne and there received and heard the emissaries of Abd ar Rahman, son of King Abulat. After twenty or more days there he traveled to Aachen to spend the winter.[45]

27. The emperor had discreetly bidden the emissaries of the king of the Saracens to precede him as he went thither. When they arrived, they waited almost three months. But since his delay had already wearied them, they went away with the emperor's consent. While he was still in that palace he received a man named Nicephorus, who came as an emissary of Leo, the emperor of Constantinople. There was also a delegation from the regions of the Dalmatians, Ro-

mans, and Slavs to continue friendship and alliance. But since neither these nor Chadalo,[46] prefect of the regions, were prompt, and since these things could not be adjusted without them, Albigarius[47] was sent to Dalmatia with Chadalo, chieftain of the regions, to conclude and arrange peace.[48] In the same year, when the sons of Godefrid, formerly king of the Northmen, had been pressed by Heriold, they sent legates to seek peace from the emperor. The legation was repudiated by him as unworthy and feigned, and aid was given instead to Heriold against them. On the Nones of February[49] that year, at the second hour of the night, the moon failed. An unnatural cluster of comets appeared in the sign of Sagittarius. Pope Stephen closed his last day[50] in the third month after he had returned to Rome from Frankland. Paschal[51] came to the Roman pontifical throne in his stead. After the solemn consecration was performed, he sent deputies to the emperor with an explanatory letter and extensive favors, intimating that not by his own effort or desire, but by popular choice and acclamation, he had fallen, rather than leaped, into this dignity. The leader of the deputation was the *nomenclator* Theodore, who returned after the business was transacted and the requests granted, namely, the confirmation of an alliance of friendship according to the custom of their[52] predecessors.

28:1. Later in the same year, the period of Lent being almost over, on the fifth feria of the last week (the day on which the memorial of the Lord's Supper is celebrated)[53] and after all things had been performed which the solemnity of so high a day required, it came to pass that, when the emperor sought to withdraw from the church to his royal residence, the lower parts of the wooden colonnade through which he had to go, weakened by decay and age and rotten with continual moisture, cracked and collapsed under the feet of the emperor and his counts. Great terror struck the entire palace with the noise of the crash, everyone fearing that the impact of that fall might have crushed the emperor. But he was protected from the immediate crisis by God to Whom he was a beloved son. For although twenty or more counts fell to the ground with him and met with various mishaps, he incurred no more regrettable damage than a hurt on his stomach where the hilt of his sword hit him and a very small skin-scratch on the lobe of his ear. His leg was also struck near the groin by the same wood, but aid was brought to him very quickly. Summoning skillful physicians, he was restored to his former health in a very short time. Twenty days later[54] indeed he went hunting at Nijmegen.

28:2. When that sport was completed the emperor held a general assembly at Aachen where he vigorously declared how much ardor for divine worship he bore in the depth of his heart. The bishops and the noblest clergy of holy church being assembled, he caused the compilation and publication of a book embodying a standard for the canonical life,[55] in which is contained the perfection of that entire order, as one upon reflection acknowledges.[56] In it Louis even ordered to be mentioned the sum, the total amount, of food and drink and of all necessities, so that everyone who served Christ in this order, men as well as nuns, being distracted by no needs, might with unhindered service remember to represent all men before the Lord. This book he distributed throughout all the cities and monasteries of canonical order in his domain by the hands of wise men, who were to cause it to be copied in all the aforesaid places and who were to obtain the cost due and assessed to be paid. This af-

forded the church a great occasion for rejoicing and constituted for the most pious emperor a deathless memorial of due
praise.[57] Likewise the emperor, beloved of God, confirmed
Benedict[58] as abbot and appointed with him monks of reso-
lute life to come and go through all monasteries and to
entrust everywhere to men and nuns alike a uniform and
unalterable manner of living according to the *Rule* of Saint
Benedict.[59]

28:3. The most pious emperor also, deeming that servants
of Christ ought not be obliged to human servitude, but
observing that the greed of many men misused the ministry
of the church for their own profit, decreed that whosoever
of servile status, recommended by learning and honesty of
character, was to be admitted to the ministry of the altar,
be first manumitted by the particular lords,[60] whether
secular or ecclesiastical, and only then be invested with the
ranks of the altar. Desiring moreover that each church have
its own revenues lest through want divine services be
neglected, he inserted in the aforesaid injunction an order
that for each church one homestead [61] be assigned with
lawful compensation, with both male and female servants.
This was the sacred emperor's exercise, this his daily pastime,
this his sport, seeing that the state might shine more illus-
triously in holy teaching and work, and that he might advance higher who in emulation of Christ humbles himself
as a poor man in like humility. For it was finally decreed at
that time that girdles adorned with golden belts and jeweled
daggers be laid aside by bishops and clerics and that fine
clothes and spurs on the ankles be abandoned. It was reckoned monstrous if a representative of the church's household should aspire to the accouterments of worldly glory.

29:1. The Enemy of mankind did not endure this holy

and worthy devotion of the emperor to God, but pursued
him everywhere and declared war against him in all the
ranks of the church. He also undertook to oppose Louis, as
the latter attacked him, with an abundance of forces and
through his members[62] to harass Christ's brave warrior
with what power and craft he could command. After these
matters had been arranged properly, the emperor later in
the same diet desired his firstborn son, Lothair, to be
recognized and designated as co-emperor, and sent his other
two sons, Pepin and Louis, to Aquitaine and Bavaria respectively, so that the people might know whose authority
to obey. But there was immediately reported to him the
defection of the Obotrites who had joined in friendship
with the sons of Godefrid and who were harassing Saxony
beyond the Elbe. With God's favor the emperor, directing
adequate forces against them, checked their movements.
Thereafter he entered the forest of the Vosges to hunt. The
hunt there was completed after the manner of the Franks,
and Louis returned to spend the winter at Aachen.

29:2. It was announced that his nephew, Bernard, in whose
behalf he had been Charles's chief adviser in making him
king of Italy, had been maddened by the counsels of evil
men to such a degree that he deserted him, that all the cities
of the realm and the princes of Italy had conspired at this
pretense, and that all the passes by which one has access
to Italy they had closed with barriers and guard-posts. When
Louis had ascertained this through messengers who informed
him, especially Bishop Rathaldus[63] and Suppo,[64] he went as
far as Châlon with a great number of troops, forces having
been procured from both Gaul and Germany. But when
Bernard observed that he himself was unequal in strength
and unsuited for the things undertaken (many of his troops

were daily falling away from him since matters had become desperate), he came to the emperor and laying down his arms prostrated himself at the emperor's feet, acknowledging that he had acted falsely. His magnates followed his example and also submitted to Louis's power and judgment, laying aside their arms. The questioning of the nobles betrayed how and why they had begun the rebellion, for what purpose they had sought to effect the things thus begun, and whom they alleged to have been their accomplices. The authors of this plot were Eggideo, chief of the royal friends;[65] Reginherius, formerly a count of the emperor's palace and a son of Count Meginherius;[66] also Reginhardus, provost of the royal chamber.[67] A great many clerics and laymen were implicated in the crime, among whom the stormy tempest involved some bishops, Anselm of Milan, Wulfold of Cremona,[68] and Theodulf of Orléans.[69]

30:1. After the leaders of the conspiracy were carried out and placed in confinement, the emperor returned to winter at Aachen as he had previously decided. There he lingered until the holy solemnity of Easter.[70] That celebration fulfilled, he remitted the harsher sentence and decreed that Bernard, the erstwhile king, and his accomplices in the crime be deprived of their eyes, although by the law and verdict of the Franks they should have been slain with a mortal blow. Many protested and sought to be revenged upon them with the full severity of the law. Yet, despite the emperor's acting more indulgently, the doom which had been remitted was brought to effect upon some. For since Bernard and Reginherius endured the destruction of their eyes with such suffering,[71] they brought bitter death upon themselves.[72] The emperor committed to monasteries the bishops who had been implicated in this savage revolt, after they had been deposed by the remaining bishops. Of the rest, however, he ordered that none be deprived of life or maimed by amputation of members; but according to what seemed necessary by virtue of compelling guilt, he sentenced some to be exiled, others to be tonsured.

30:2. After these things, there was reported to the emperor the arrogant disobedience of the Bretons who broke out into such insolence that they dared to designate one of their own number, Murman, as king, and they refused subjection to the emperor in every manner. To avenge their impudence the emperor departed and advanced to the frontiers of the Bretons, assembling a military force from all sides. After a general assembly at Vannes, he entered the province and with little time and effort plundered everything, until Murman was killed by a certain keeper of the royal horses named Choslus while he was attacking the baggage-train. All Brittany fell with him and surrendered, agreeing to whatever conditions the emperor imposed, namely, to be enslaved anew. For as many of whatever rank were demanded as hostages were given and received, and the entire land was disposed according to his will.

31. From those Breton frontiers the emperor then withdrew and revisited the city of Angers, where Queen Irmingard lay, worn by prolonged loss of blood. She survived only two days after the emperor's return, dying on the third day, the fifth before the Nones of October.[73] (In that year an eclipse of the sun had occurred on the eighth day before the Ides of July.)[74] The obsequies of the queen were performed and the emperor betook himself by a direct route through the city of Rouen and of Amiens to winter-quarters at Aix. As he returned and entered the palace of Heristal, emissaries of Sigo, the Beneventan duke, met

him and presented expensive gifts and justified their master in the death of his predecessor, Grimoald. There were present emissaries of other peoples, of the Obotrites, Godu-scani,[75] and Timotiani,[76] who had recently attached themselves to us, abandoning their alliance with the Bulgars. Also present there were emissaries of Liudevitus,[77] ruler of lower Pannonia, who accused Cadalus (falsely as was afterward clear) of wreaking his cruelty upon them. When these had been heard, appeased, and sent away, the emperor removed into the palace to winter according to plan. While he was staying there, Sclaomir, king of the Obotrites, was delivered to him by the Saxon dukes. Since he was accused of defection and was not able to answer the charges, he was sentenced to banishment and his kingdom was given to Ceadragus,[78] son of Trasco.

32:1. At the same time a certain Basque, Lupus, surnamed "of Centullus," [79] rose in rebellion and provoked Werinus, count of Auvergne, and Berengar[80] of Toulouse to battle. Along with many others, Lupus lost his brother Gersandus, but he himself escaped by flight. Afterwards, brought before the emperor and commanded to state his case, he was subdued by reason and condemned to exile. During that winter the emperor convened at the palace a public assembly of his people. He listened to reports from his entire realm by emissaries whom he had sent out to restore the fallen or strengthen the persisting estate of holy church. Whatever he adjudged profitable, he expanded (holy devotion impelling him); he left nothing untried that seemed to advance the honor of God's holy church. In the meanwhile, to the laws in which public matters seemed to be defective, certain chapters were added which to this day are retained as quite indispensable.

32:2. On the advice of his men he began to think about entering the marital state again. For many feared that he might relinquish the helms of the kingdom. Finally satisfying their wish and inspecting the daughters of nobles brought before him from all districts, he married Judith, daughter of Welf, a right noble count.[81] When summer came his people assembled with him in the palace at Ingelheim. There he received the messengers of his armies which had been dispatched to suppress the overt treachery of Liudevitus. But the same difficulty remained almost impossible. On the contrary, indeed, instead of restraint, Liudevitus, inflated with a swelling of arrogance, demanded certain conditions of the emperor through his emissaries: if the emperor would fulfill them, he himself would in turn obey his commands as formerly. But they were scorned and refused by the emperor as unworthy. Liudevitus, therefore, intending to remain firm in his perfidy, allied to himself in his perfidy whomever he could. After the return of the armies from the frontiers of Pannonia, and while Liudevitus continued in his treachery, Cadolach, duke of Friuli, fell ill with a fever and brought his day to an end,[82] and Baldricus succeeded in his place. As soon as the latter came into the province and entered the regions of Carinthia,[83] he routed the forces of Liudevitus near the Drave river with a few of his own men, and driving away the remainder, compelled all to withdraw from his frontiers. Liudevitus, put to flight by Baldricus, met Borna,[84] duke of Dalmatia, who was encamped near the Kulpa river. Borna, left in the lurch by the treachery (or by the terror—which is uncertain) of the Goduscani, but aided by a private auxiliary force of his own men, safely escaped the impending crisis and later crushed the deserters.

32:3. In the ensuing winter Liudevitus again invaded Dalmatia, trying to ravage everything, slaying with the sword what was animate, consigning to fire what was inanimate. Since Borna could not meet him with force, he sought to do harm by craft. He did not declare open war on Liudevitus, but with unexpected assaults he crushed him and his army to such a degree that it caused Liudevitus shame and regret to have attempted such things. For with three thousand of his army killed and horses and various large apparatus belonging to him destroyed, he was forced by Borna to abandon the region. All these things the emperor heard gladly while he was at Aix. In the meanwhile the Basques, seething with the native plague of sedition, were so completely tamed in that very year by Pepin, the emperor's son, that none of them dared rebel. His father had of course dispatched him for that purpose. When these reports had been made, the emperor dismissed the assembly. He gave his attention to hunting for a suitable time in the Ardennes, then returned to the palace of Aix to spend the winter.

33. As winter approached, the emperor caused an assembly of the people to be convened at the palace. Borna, complaining of the hostility of Liudevitus, received from the emperor great forces of assistance with which he could obliterate the land of his foe. At first the forces, divided into three groups,[85] laid waste with sword and fire almost all the land of the hostile domain. Liudevitus defended himself in a certain very lofty fortress, going out neither to fight nor to treat. After Borna's men had returned home, the people of Carniola and certain of them of Carinthia, who had attached themselves to Liudevitus, surrendered to our Duke Baldricus. At this assembly also Bera, count of

Barcelona, accused by a man named Sanila[86] and charged with faithlessness, met Sanila in knightly combat,[87] according to their own law (since each was a Goth) and lost. Although by law punishment should have been imposed upon him, that is, sentenced to death he should have been slain as one guilty of high treason, he was nevertheless granted his life by the emperor's clemency and was ordered to settle in Rouen. It was then announced that thirteen pirate ships had come by sea from the settlements of Northland and were putting ashore to pillage our frontiers. The emperor gave command that watchtowers and guardposts be constructed against them. They were accordingly repulsed from Flemish soil and at the same time from the mouth of the Seine. But they turned against Aquitaine where they ravaged a village named Bouin and from which they returned laden with booty.

34:1. In this year the Lord Emperor spent the winter season in Aachen. In the month of February [821] an assembly was celebrated at Aix. Three battalions were dispatched to lay waste the land of Liudevitus. War was also declared on Abulat, king of the Saracens, since the imaginary peace which he had ostensibly agreed to was broken. On the Kalends of May[88] the emperor held another assembly at Nijmegen, at which he caused the partition of the realm (which he had long ago made among his sons) to be read publicly and to be confirmed by all the nobles who were then present. There also he received, heard, and sent back the emissaries of Pope Paschal, Peter,[89] bishop of Civitavecchia, and Leo the *nomenclator*.[90] Departing thence the emperor revisited Aachen. Afterwards passing through the Ardennes up to the height of Remiremont and the broad waste of the Vosges, he spent the remaining half of summer and the

autumn. In the midst of these events, Borna lost his life
and the emperor designated as successor his nephew Lada-
slav.[91] He received also a message of the death of Leo,
emperor of Constantinople, who had been murdered by his
servants, in particular by Michael,[92] who was appointed
in his place by agreement of the fellow-conspirators and
especially the pretorian soldiers.

34:2. In mid-October a public assembly was convoked
at Thionville. There the Lord Emperor, with solemn pomp,
joined in marriage Irmingard, daughter of Count Hugo,[93]
to his first-born son Lothair. There were also present
legates of the Roman pontiff, Theodore, the administrative
chief, and Florus,[94] with a great many varied gifts. Moreover, although the emperor's clemency always shone won-
derfully in different matters, in this assembly, it became
most manifestly evident how extraordinarily great[95] it was
in his heart. For all those who had conspired against his
life and kingdom were recalled. He not only granted
them life and limb, but also with great display of magnanimity restored the possessions of which they had been
lawfully deprived. Adalard,[96] one-time abbot of the monastery of Corbie, but at that time living in the monastery
of Saint Filibert, he restored to his former office. Likewise
Adalard's brother, Bernarius,[97] summoned from the monastery of Saint Benedict and reconciled, Louis restored to
the same place along with Adalard. These affairs having
been accomplished and other things which advantage demanded having been executed, he sent his son Lothair to
winter at Worms, while he himself returned to Aachen.

35:1. In the year following the Lord Emperor ordered a
general assembly to meet in a place the name of which is
Attigny. Thither bishops, abbots, and spiritual men, and

also the nobles of his realm were summoned for counsel. The emperor sought eagerly first to be reconciled to his brothers whom he had caused to be unwillingly tonsured, then to all those on whom it appeared that some injury had been inflicted. Thereafter acknowledging openly that he had sinned and imitating the example of the Emperor Theodosius,[98] he undertook a voluntary penance as much for those deeds as for the injuries which he had done to his nephew Bernard. He also set aright whatever he could discover had been done amiss anywhere by himself or by his father by largesse of alms as well as by the urgent prayers of Christ's servants and also by his own personal reparation. He was careful to appease the Godhead as though these things, which had befallen each one according to law, had been done by his own cruelty.

35:2. On the same occasion, however, he sent an army from Italy into Pannonia against Liudevitus. Not able to remain there, Liudevitus abandoned his own state, and going to a certain prince of Dalmatia was taken by him into the latter's city. When the situation was thus altered, Liudevitus weakened his rescuer by guile and subjected the city to his own domination. And although he would neither risk battle with us nor engage in talks, he nonetheless declared to the legates that he had erred and he promised to come to the Lord Emperor.

35:3. It was at the same time announced to the emperor that the guardians of the Spanish border had crossed the river Segre, had penetrated the interior of Spain, and had happily returned with great booty after all the cities which had offered resistance to them had been laid waste and burned. Those also who were defending the Breton frontiers, having invaded Brittany, had devastated the region with sword and torch, because of an insurrection of a certain Breton named Wiomarchus.[99] Following this accomplishment they too returned joyfully. This diet was then brought to an end and the Lord Emperor sent his son Lothair into Italy with his kinsman Wala, a monk, as well as with Geruncus, the *ostiarius*.[100] By their counsel he adjusted, arranged, and repaired the public as well as the private affairs of the Italian kingdom. When Louis had decided to send his son Pepin to Aquitaine, he first joined to him in marriage the daughter of Count Theotbert.[101] Thereafter he directed him to rule the aforementioned areas. Disposing of these matters, he devoted the season of autumn to hunting, according to the custom of Frankish kings. In order to winter beyond the Rhine he sought the place which is called Frankfurt. There he ordered an assembly of the neighboring nations to be convoked, that is, of all those living beyond the waves of the Rhine who conform to the sovereignty of the Franks. Treating with them of all things profitable, he made suitable provision for the affairs of each. In the same assembly there was present an embassy of Avars bringing gifts. Ambassadors of the Northmen renewing and confirming peace were not wanting. When he had heard them with due ceremony and sent them away, he wintered in that place, the buildings having been equipped with new and worthy fortifications suitable to the season.

36. In the same villa, that is, Frankfurt, in the month of May when winter was past, the emperor held an assembly of Southern Franks, Saxons, and other peoples along the borders. He adjusted with fitting result a contest of two brothers disputing with great contention between themselves[102] about the kingship. Wilzi by stock, sons of Liubi,

the former king, their names were Mileguastus and Celead-ragus.[103] When their father Liubi had declared war on the Obotrites, he had been killed and the kingship was transmitted to the first-born. But when he exhibited himself in royal administration as immeasurably more sluggish than conditions required, the good will of the people turned to the younger brother. When the contest came to the emperor's attention, the will of the people was sought and discovered, and the younger one was forthwith declared the prince. At length the emperor sent them both away dowered with ample gifts, bound by oaths, and friendly to each other and to him. In the meanwhile, Lothair, the Lord Emperor's son, had been sent by his father to Italy, as noted above,[104] and had arranged for negotiations in accordance with the advice of the men who had been sent with him. Although some things had been achieved, others were still unsettled and he was considering how to reply concerning each to his father after his return. At Pope Paschal's urgent request he had gone to Rome for the holy solemnity of Easter.[105] Acknowledged by the pope on that holy day with stately pomp, he received the imperial diadem at Saint Peter's together with the title *Augustus*. Later, when he had come to Pavia, weighty necessities constrained him to delay there. It was therefore in the month of June before he finally approached his father to announce the things achieved and to inquire about the things unfinished. To complete what had been less well accomplished, Adalhard, count of the palace,[106] was dispatched with Mauringus as his associate. Gundulf,[107] bishop of Metz, died about the same time and all the clergy and people of that church, as though animated by one spirit,[108] demanded as their priest the emperor's brother Drogo[109] who was living most honorably in the canonical habit. In a marvelous manner the agreement of emperor, his nobles, and the entire people, as though united by a certain bond, conspired so that all were found to consent and none to dissent.[110] The emperor, therefore, with surpassing joy, acceded to the church's request and gave them the pontiff whom they sought. In the same assembly the death of the tyrant Liudevitus, slain by craft, was announced. The emperor dissolved this diet and authorized another assembly at Compiègne in the autumn.

37:1. At this time, moreover, it was related to the emperor that Theodore, an administrative chief of the holy Roman church, and Leo the *nomenclator* had been deprived of their eyes and thereafter beheaded in the bishop's Lateran palace. Jealousy was immediately spawned in the murderers, because it was said that they who had been killed had suffered for their fealty to Lothair. The pontiff's fame was also injured since the murder was attributed to his connivance. While the emperor was preparing to send Adalungus, abbot of the monastery of Saint Vaast, and Count Hunfred of Chur,[111] to investigate the matter very thoroughly, the emissaries of Pope Paschal arrived, John, bishop of Selva Candida, and Benedict, archdeacon of the holy Roman church, offering an excuse to answer the accusation,[112] and bringing the emperor an account of the inquiry. After they had been heard and dismissed with suitable reply, he bade his designated emissaries to go on to Rome as ordered, to determine the truth of doubtful matters. After several delays, however, he came, as seemed proper, to Compiègne at the appointed time, that is, on the Kalends of November.[113] To this diet the legates dispatched to Rome came back, announcing that Pope Paschal had by oath purged himself and a great many bishops of the death of the murdered men, but had been unable to deliver up the murderers, strongly asserting that those who had been killed had suffered with just deserts. Together with themselves they presented emissaries sent by the Apostolic Lord who reported like things. The names of the legates are John, bishop of Selva Candida, Sergius the librarian, Quirinus the subdeacon, and Leo master of troops. The emperor, therefore, most merciful by nature and not able to pursue further a vindication of the slain, although strongly wishing to do so, decided to desist from inquiry of this kind and dismissed the Roman emissaries with suitable replies.

37:2. In the same season certain strange signs were appearing which disturbed the emperor's mind, in particular an earthquake at the palace of Aix, unheard-of sounds in the nighttime, the fasting of a certain girl who abstained absolutely from all food for twelve months, abundant and unaccustomed lightnings, the falling of stones along with hail, and plagues of men and beasts.[114] Because of these singular occurrences the most pious emperor advised that fasts should be observed frequently and that the Godhead should be appeased by urgent prayers of the priests and by liberality of alms, declaring that by these prodigies a great future calamity was most assuredly portended for the human race. In the month of June a son was born to him of Queen Judith, whom at the time of baptism he was pleased to name Charles.[115] In the same year Counts Eblus and Asenarius[116] were ordered to proceed across the peaks of the Pyrenean mountain range. When they had gone with great hosts to Pamplona and, the business accomplished, were returning thence, they experienced the usual treachery of the place and the innate deceit of the inhabitants.[117]

For ambushed by the natives of that place and all their troops having been lost, they fell into the hands of the enemies. The captors sent Eblus to Córdoba to the king of the Saracens, but spared Asenarius since he was related to them by consanguinity.[118]

38. In the meanwhile, when Lothair, sent by his father as noted above,[119] had come to Rome, he was received most lavishly by Pope Eugenius.[120] He complained of those things which had befallen, namely, why those who had been loyal to the emperor and the Franks had been destroyed with unjust and violent death; why those who had survived had been held a laughing-stock to the rest; why also such serious charges were cried out against the Roman pontiffs and judges. It was discovered that the estates of many had been unjustly confiscated, either by the ignorance or idleness of certain pontiffs, and also by the blind and rapacious greed of the judges. Therefore, by restoring what things had been wrongfully taken away, Lothair caused great joy for the Roman people. It was moreover decreed, according to ancient custom, that there be sent from the emperor's side those who, in the exercise of judicial authority, would execute justice for all the people and would weigh with equal balance[121] at a time when it would seem fitting to the emperor. When the son returned and related these things to the father, the emperor, lover of equity and devotee of truth, was drenched with great joy because comfort and affection had appeared for those unlawfully oppressed.

39:1. At a later season the Lord Emperor ordered an assembly of his own people to be convoked in the month of May at Aachen.[122] While it was in session, a legation of Bulgars (who, according to his decree, had long dwelt in Bavaria) was presented to him to be heard. The legation was there for the purpose of determining the precise limits of the boundaries to be observed between Bulgars and Franks after the peace settlement. There were present also not a few nobles of the Bretons, professing with many words submission and compliance.[123] Among them was Wiemarchus, who outranked the others in importance and who with mad heedlessness and very rash daring had rushed into so much that he had provoked even the emperor to make an expedition to his regions to quell his arrogance. When he had declared that he repented of his action and had professed his allegiance to the emperor, he was mercifully received by the emperor, according to his manner, with the clemency which he was always accustomed to practice. Dowered with gifts, Wiemarchus and his fellow-citizens were allowed to return to their native soil. Yet later, not forgetting his traditional perfidy but entirely forgetting all the good things which he had promised and which he had experienced, he continued to attack his neighbors, the emperor's loyal subjects, and to harass them with unremitting ills. At length it came to pass that, overpowered by Lantbert's men, he received life's end with the fate of all evil men (as luck would have it) in his own house.

39:2. The emissaries of the Bulgars as well as the Bretons having been dismissed, the emperor retired to the remotenesses of the Vosges for an exercise of hunting, believing that it was convenient to do that again until he returned to Aachen in the month of August according to a general promise to the people. At that season he gave command that the peace which was requested by the Northmen be confirmed in the month of October. Everything having been completed and determined in the diet according to decree, he himself with his son Lothair departed to Nijmegen, the younger Louis having been sent away to Bavaria. When the autumn hunt was over, he came back to the palace of Aix at the beginning of winter. After the Bulgar emissaries returned from that assembly[124] with the emperor's letters, their king received what had been written not at all graciously, because he had not obtained what he sought. Therefore, with a certain sullenness, sending the same messenger back, he demanded that a common boundary or frontier be fixed or with whatever power he was able he would maintain the limits of his own frontiers. But when gossip had spread the report that the king making such demands was absent from the realm, the emperor detained the legate until through Bertricus, count of the palace, he found that what was being rumored was false. When the truth was learned, he sent the emissary away with the matter still unfinished.

40:1. On the Kalends of February[125] Pepin, son of the emperor, approached his father who was wintering at Aix. He returned after he had been cautioned by the emperor to be ready to cope with any revolt which might arise from the regions of Spain. On the Kalends of the month of June[126] the emperor came to Ingelheim. There an assembly of his own people met him as he had ordered. In the same diet, according to his custom, he admonished, decreed, and defined many things profitable to the church, and received, heard, dismissed embassies presented to him from the holy Roman see and from Abbot Dominic of Ölberg. Moreover, since two dukes, Ceadragus of the Obotrites and Tunglo of the Sorbs, were accused and the trial did not appear sufficiently clear, he sent them back to their own

lands under censure. Heriold also came from the regions of
Northland with his wife and no small band of Danes.
Together with his family he was drenched in the wave
of holy baptism at Mainz at Saint Alban's church[127] and
afterwards was dowered by the emperor with many gifts.
Fearing that because of such action a dwelling-place might
be denied Heriold on his native soil, the most pious emperor gave him a certain county in Frisia named Rüstringen.
Thither he could betake himself and his followers in safety
if necessity should require. In the meanwhile when Baldricus
and Gerald and other guardians of the Pannonian frontiers
presented themselves, Baldricus introduced to the emperor a
certain presbyter George, a man of exemplary life, who
stated that he could construct an organ in the Greek
fashion. The emperor received him graciously. Because
God had endowed George with those faculties which were
hitherto unusual in the Frankish realm before him, the
emperor gave thanks and commended him to Tanculf, chief
of the sacred fisc,[128] ordering the treasurer to care for
George out of the public revenues and commanding him
to make available whatever was needed for this work.[129]

40:2. In the meantime, in the middle of October, he
commanded a Germanic assembly to gather beyond the
Rhine in a village named Salz.[130] As it was in session, the
treachery and defection of Aizo[131] was reported. He had
fled from the palace of the Lord Emperor to the city of
Vich. Having been admitted there he overthrew Roda
and inflicted no little damage upon those who were trying
to resist. The citadels which he could force he fortified
strongly, assigning garrisons to them. Moreover, Aizo's
brother, having been sent to the king of the Saracens,
Abd ar Rahman, received a powerful and courageous army

for use against us. These matters of course moved and stirred the emperor's mind to revenge. Thinking, however, that nothing should be done hastily, he decided that the opinion of his councilors should make known what was needful in such a case. About the same time Hilduin,[132] abbot of the monastery of blessed Denis, sent monks to Rome as bearers of a petition to Eugenius, prelate of the holy Roman see, begging that the bones of the blessed martyr Sebastian be conveyed to him. The Apostolic Lord, fulfilling his desire, sent the booty of Christ's most consecrated soldier by the aforesaid emissaries. They were received in devout manner by the abbot and were placed together with the portable casket, just as they were brought, next to the body of blessed Médard. While they remained there, God granted so great an abundance of miracles to mortals through their prompt aid that the multitude of miracles exceeds number. Henceforth let quality cause faith to abound, unless faith be placed in those ears which have been persuaded to oppose nothing to divine command, but "all things are possible to him who believes." [133]

41:1. In the meanwhile Aizo attacked those who were settling within our borders and laid waste Cerdagne and the region of Valles as far as his cruelty advanced. He was aided by auxiliary troops of Moors and Saracens so adequately that some of our men were forced to abandon citadels and towns which they had hitherto held, and a great many even forsook us and joined themselves to their confederacy. Among them Willemund, son of Bera, together with many of his associates, joined their treachery. Impelled to check them and to strengthen our men,[134] the emperor, while he was setting in order an army, dispatched in advance Abbot Helisachar,[135] Count Hildebrand, and

Donatus. Going ahead, with forces of Goths and Spaniards, they steadfastly withstood Aizo's violence, Count Bernard of Barcelona[136] succeeding spectacularly in reducing the rebel efforts to naught. Observing this, Aizo departed to seek a pretorian army from the Saracens. Obtaining it together with its chief, Abu Marvan, Aizo marched to Saragossa and thence right up to Barcelona. Immediately the emperor dispatched against them his son, King Pepin of Aquitaine, and his personal emissaries, Counts Hugo and Matfrid.[137] These, however, advanced more slowly than was fitting, delays were added to delays[138] as long as possible, until the Saracens had captured Saragossa and devastated the district about Barcelona and Gerona. Just before this defeat, to be sure, occurred those frightful rays during the nighttime, glowing red with human gore and blazing with brightness of fire.[139] After receiving the yearly gifts at Compiègne, the emperor learning about these events, ordered forces to protect the March mentioned above, and then until the wintry season hastened to a hunt in the forests near Compiègne and Kierzy.

41:2. In the month of August [827], Pope Eugenius closed his final day on earth. Valentinus,[140] a deacon, succeeded in his place. Since he survived scarcely a month, Gregory,[141] presbyter of the title of Saint Mark, was chosen in his stead, the consecration being deferred until a conference with the emperor. When the latter gave consent and approved the choice of clergy and people, the new pope was ordained in the place of the former. In the month of September in the same year, legates of the Emperor Michael arrived at Compiègne bringing gifts. Received honorably, attended most splendidly, dowered liberally, they also departed favorably. In that very year Einhard,[142] most prudent man of his time, inflamed with ardor of holy devotion, sent to Rome, and with the pope's consent caused the bodies of Saints Marcellinus and Peter to be translated to Frankland. He enshrined them very appropriately in his own domain and at his own expense. By their merits even yet the Lord is working many valuable miracles there.[143]

42:1. In the month of February of the ensuing year, a public assembly was held at Aachen, where discussion boiled very heatedly about the injury and shame recently occurring in other places and especially in the Spanish March. The matter having been aired and plainly investigated, men who had been appointed dukes by the emperor were discovered as authors of this crime.[144] The emperor therefore gave order that, with dignities stripped away, they atone for this crime of negligence. And in similar manner, when it was charged and proven against Baldricus, duke of Friuli, that by his cowardice and carelessness our territory was laid waste by the Bulgars, he was deprived of his duchy and authority over it was divided among four counts. Of course the emperor's mind, by nature very merciful, was always eager to solicit clemency for the erring ones. Yet they to whom errors were the distinguishing marks misused his clemency for further cruelty. It will afterwards become clear[145] in what manner they brought against him the greatest slaughter of which they were capable in return for the blessing of life.

42:2. At that time Halitgar,[146] bishop of Cambrai, and Ansfrid, abbot of the monastery of Nonantola, returned from regions beyond the seas and reported that they had been most nobly received by Michael.[147] The emperor wisely held a public assembly at Ingelheim during the ensuing summer. There he received, then dismissed, the emissaries of the Roman pope. Quirinus the administrative chief and Theophylact the *nomenclator* who had come with rich gifts. As soon as he had arrived at Thionville and heard the rumor that the Saracens were about to enter our frontiers, he dispatched his son Lothair to the March with many strong hosts of Franks. When the father arrived at Lyons with his paternal commands and stood ready to receive a messenger from the Spanish regions, Lothair's brother Pepin approached to have a conference. And while they were delaying there, the emissary returned, saying, "The Saracens and Moors have indeed moved as large an army as possible, but we have halted the advance and the enemy can proceed no further into our borders." [148] These things having been heard, Pepin returned to Aquitaine, but Lothair to his father.

42:3. In the meantime the sons of Godefrid, late king of the Danes, had driven Heriold from the kingdom. Although the emperor wanted to aid Heriold, he had renewed a truce with Godefrid's sons. The Saxon counts therefore having been sent against them along with Heriold himself, Louis gave order that they treat with the sons of Godefrid on the basis of their receiving Heriold in partnership as formerly. But without our knowledge Heriold, impatient with these delays, burned some of their villas with "Greek fire" [149] and carried away booty. Supposing that this had been done with our consent, they pressed upon our men who were unprepared and who were suspecting no such occurrence. Crossing the river Eider, they fell upon our encampment, put it to flight, and took possession of everything before returning to their own camp. But afterwards discovering the truth and fearing due vengeance, they acknowledged their mistake, sending messengers first to those on whom they had inflicted such damage, then to the emperor. Thereafter they made suitable satisfaction according to the emperor's will in order that the peace might remain unrent. The emperor favored them in proportion to the vow and request.

42:4. Count Boniface,[150] the emperor's prefect of the island of Corsica, entered a small ship with his brother Berald [151] and others, and while he was ranging the seas searching for pirates but not finding them, he came ashore on the islands of the Sardinians who were friendly to him. There taking on others who were familiar with the sea-route, he sailed to Africa and landed between Utica and Carthage. Against him a throng of Africans converged and attacked five times. Five times they were beaten off, losing a great number of men, although they happened to encounter[152] those of our men whom either great speed or ill-advised lightness compelled to dare too much. When Boniface therefore embarked in the vessels with his allies and turned back to his native land, he left to the Africans an unsatisfied and hitherto unheard-of fear. In that year a fading of the moon occurred twice, once on the Kalends of July and once on the night of the Lord's Nativity.[153] Moreover a certain supply of grain was brought to the emperor from the region of Gascony, smaller than wheat but not polished as peas, which was said to have fallen from the sky.[154] The Lord Emperor spent the winter season at Aix.

43. When winter was over, while the sacred days of Lent were being observed and the reverend solemnity of Easter was approaching,[155] there was on an unseasonable night

an earthquake so severe that it threatened ruin to every
building. A violent wind followed close thereafter and
shook not only the smaller ones, but also the palace of Aix
itself, so vehemently that it uncovered the greater part of
heavy leaden tiles with which the basilica of Saint Mary
Mother of God had been roofed. The emperor was detained
in that place by a great many compelling necessities and
public services. He decided to set forth thence on the
Kalends of July[156] and to hasten to Worms to take part in
a general assembly of the people in August. A rumor
forced him to change this decision in some degree, a rumor
which held that the Northmen intended to violate the
truce, cross the frontiers, and lay waste the region beyond
the Elbe. But since they were restraining themselves, the
emperor went on according to the appointed place and
time, dealt eagerly with those matters which appeared, received the yearly donations, and sent his son Lothair to
Italy. At that assembly he learned that all around him the
secret machinations of those whose life he had spared were
crawling like a crab and were inciting the minds of many
persons through certain underground devices. He therefore
determined to erect a special bulwark against them. He
set Bernard, hitherto count of the parts and borders of the
Spains, in charge of his chamber. That action did not put
an end to the hotbed of discord, but rather gave it increase.[157]
Those who were being consumed with so great a disease
could not as yet betray their sore since no forces came
to aid them in accomplishing what they longed for. They
determined for that reason to defer their plans until another
time. The emperor, however, with these things disentangled
as occasion dictated, crossed the Rhine, came to the villa

of Frankfurt, and there engaged in hunting as long as seemed good and as long as the approaching frosts of winter allowed. About Martinmas he returned to Aachen to celebrate that feast, and Saint Andrew's, as well as the Lord's Nativity along with the rest.[158]

PART III (CHAPTERS 44-64): A.D. 830-40

Chapter 44:1. Later, during the Lenten season,[1] while the emperor was traveling through the places lying close to the sea, the chiefs of the evil faction,[2] not willing to delay any longer, displayed the sore which had been hidden for a while. First, the great nobles contrived among themselves a league, then attached the lesser ones to them. Part of them was always desirous of change after the manner of greedy dogs and birds which look for another's defeat to add to their satiety.[3] Relying therefore upon the number and consent of many, they approached the emperor's son Pepin, alleging his being slighted, Bernard's arrogance, and the despising of others, and claiming indeed (what is wicked to relate)[4] that Bernard was an incestuous[5] polluter of Pepin's father's bed. They insinuated furthermore that his father was baffled by certain delusions[6] to such a degree that he was in no way able to avenge these things nor indeed even to perceive them. It was therefore necessary, they said, that a good son suffer his father's shame with indignation and that he restore his father to reason and honor. Not only would a reputation for virtue pursue the one doing this, they asserted, but also an extension of his earthly realm—by this remark dissembling their guilt.[7] The young man, therefore, enticed by these incentives, proceeded with them and with many of their troops to Verberie by way of the city of Orléans, since Odo had been removed from that place and Matfrid had been reinstated.[8] But when the emperor learned with absolute certainty about the deadly armed conspiracy against himself, his wife, and Bernard, he allowed Bernard to protect himself by flight. He requested his wife, however, to remain in Laon and to settle in the monastery of Saint Mary; but he himself hastened to Compiègne.

44:2. Those who came to Verberie with Pepin (Warinus and Lantbert having been dispatched along with as many others as possible) caused Queen Judith to be brought before them from the city and basilica of the monastery. Threatening death by torture, they compelled her to promise that, if ample opportunity were given her to speak to the emperor, she would persuade him to devote himself to a monastery, laying aside his arms and having his hair shorn, and that she herself would also do similarly, placing the veil upon her head. The more eagerly they desired this procedure, the more easily they put credence in her acquiescence. Sending some of their men with her, they brought her to the emperor. When he had given her permission to speak more privately, he allowed her to take the veil in order to escape death, but he demanded time to deliberate his tonsure.[9] Since he always lived kindly toward others, the emperor was depressed by their unjust hatred which was so great that they loathed the very existence of him by whose favor they were alive and without whose favor they would have been justly and lawfully deprived of life. When the queen returned to them, they restrained themselves from other injuries indeed, but yielding to the shouting of the public, they had her carried away into exile and thrust into the monastery of Saint Radegunda.

45:1. Later, about the month of May, the emperor's son Lothair came from Italy and found him at Compiègne. As he was approaching, the entire faction hostile to the em-

peror joined itself to him. He seemed to impute nothing
dishonorable to his father at that time, yet he approved
what had been done.[10] Lastly, contrary to the emperor's
pledge, Bernard's brother Heribert[11] was sentenced to loss
of his eyes and his first cousin Odo[12] was disarmed and
sent away into exile, as if they were accomplices and pro-
moters of those things which were shouted against Bernard
and the queen. Continuing there for a while, the emperor
in name only passed the summer. But when autumn was
drawing near, those who were of contrary opinions to
the emperor wished for a general gathering to be held somewhere in Frankland. The emperor secretly resisted, dis-
trusting the Franks and entrusting himself to the Germans.
The emperor's sentiment therefore prevailed that the people
come together at Nijmegen. Fearing that the multitude
of opponents would overwhelm the paucity of his faithful
ones, he gave order that each person coming to the diet
employ a single retainer only. He enjoined Count Lambert
to have care of the frontiers reckoned to him and directed
Abbot Helisachar to exercise justice there. At length therefore the assembly gathered at Nijmegen. All Germany
flocked thither to serve as aid to the emperor. Wishing
still further to break the power of his adversaries, the
emperor accused Abbot Hilduin, asking why he approached
in a hostile manner although he had been ordered to come
alone. The latter, unable to answer satisfactorily, was forthwith commanded to leave the palace and spend the winter
with only a few men in a campaign tent near Paderborn.
Abbot Walach was commanded to retire to the monastery
of Corbie and there show himself as one bound by the Rule.

45:2. When they who had gathered to oppose the emperor observed that their forces were being depleted,[13]

they surrendered to abject hopelessness. Throughout a whole
night, assembling and meeting at the quarters of the emperor's son Lothair, they urged him either to go to war[14]
or to withdraw somewhere away from the emperor's influence. They spent the entire night in this deliberation. In
the morning the emperor ordered his son not to confide
in the common enemy, but to come to him as son to father.
Heeding these words, in spite of those around him trying
to dissuade him, he approached his father. He was not
assailed with harsh rebuke, but was chided with moderate
leniency. When Lothair entered the recesses of the royal
residence, the crowd, splitting in two by instigation of the
devil, began to rage. The fury would have mounted to
bloodshed on both sides if imperial wisdom had not been on
the watch. For while they were in an uproar and were almost
ready to rush into a mad passion, the emperor appeared
before them all with his son. Immediately the animal-like
excitement abated. When the emperor's address had been
heard, the entire popular disorder subsided. The emperor
thereupon gave command that all leaders of the wicked
conspiracy be kept under individual guard. When they
were later brought to judgment, the emperor permitted
none of them to be slain, although all the magistrates of the
law and the emperor's sons had decreed by legal decision
that they suffer the death penalty as persons guilty of
lèse-majesté. But employing, as it seemed to many, a milder
procedure than was fitting (although kindness and mercy
were his custom), he commanded the laymen to be tonsured
at suitable places and the clerics to be detained in similarly
appropriate monasteries.

46:1. When these things had been accomplished, the
emperor repaired to Aachen for the winter. Throughout the

season he kept with him his son Lothair. In the meanwhile he sent to Aquitaine and recalled his wife and her brothers, Conrad and Rudolf,[15] who had been tonsured a long time ago.[16] Yet not until she had purged herself of the charges in the manner prescribed did he again accept her with the honor due a wife.[17] After that was done, on the Purification of Saint Mary[18] he granted life to all those sentenced to death.[19] He then allowed Lothair to go to Italy, Pepin to Aquitaine, and Louis to Bavaria; but he himself kept the Lenten season and the solemnity of Easter[20] at Aachen. When the Paschal observances therefore had been completed,[21] the emperor set out to Ingelheim. Finally, not unmindful of his accustomed mercy, which, as Job says of himself, grew up with him from the beginning and seems to have emerged with him from his mother's womb,[22] summoning those whom he had dispersed throughout various localities as their offenses required, he reinstated them in their own properties. To those who had been tonsured he granted leave to remain thus or to return to their former condition as they wished. Then, after having dispatched his son Lothair to Italy, the emperor crossed through the Vosges into the district of Remiremont and there indulged in fishing and hunting as long as it was agreeable to him.

46:2. Later in the season of autumn he enjoined his people generally to gather in Thionville. At that place three legates of the Saracens (two of whom were Saracens, one a Christian) came from regions beyond the sea bearing noble gifts from their fatherland, different kinds of perfumes and garments. When peace had been sought and secured, they were sent back. Bernard was also present, who in the aforesaid manner had saved himself by flight and had lived a long while in banishment along the frontiers of Spain.

He therefore approached the emperor to seek a means of purging himself in the manner usual among the Franks, namely, to challenge the person hurling the accusation and to wipe out the charge by force of arms. But since the accuser did not present himself when summoned, the purgation was executed by oaths, weapons not being necessary. The emperor had ordered his son Pepin to appear at this diet, but the latter withheld himself from the assembly, although he did come after the diet. The emperor, thereupon wishing to chastise him for disobedience and churlishness, required him to remain with him and indeed held him at Aix until the Lord's Nativity. Pepin, however, taking it amiss to be detained against his will, resorted to flight[23] and without his father's knowledge departed to Aquitaine. The emperor continued to remain in winter quarters at Aachen as he had begun.

47. When the rigor of winter had been safely endured[24] and the approach of spring [832] was at hand, it was announced to the emperor that several movements were stirring in Bavaria. To repress them he left hurriedly, came to Augsburg, quelled the insurrections, returned without delay, and ordered a public assembly to be held in Orléans. Thither he ordered Pepin, who reluctantly came forward. Reflecting that the advice of certain evil men had corrupted his son's mind as much by threats as by promises, and fearing Bernard especially, whose counsel Pepin was at that time said to be following (for Bernard was lingering in Aquitaine), the emperor crossed the Loire and came with his retinue to Jouac le Palais in the territory of Limoges. There the case of both having been aired, Bernard was deprived of his honors since he was suspected of disloyalty, although the challenger would not come to the assembly.

But Pepin, for the correction of his vicious manners, he ordered to be brought under private guard to Trèves. Although he was conducted thither and treated very kindly, he was stealthily released at night by his own men among the guards, and until the emperor's return from Aquitaine he roved about wherever he could and would.

47:2. At that time the emperor decreed a particular division of the realm between his sons Lothair and Charles, which as a promise succumbed not a whit to extraordinary hindrances which must be related. It appeared that the emperor might withdraw from Aquitaine at a suitable time, but after a short period he convoked the people on Martinmas[25] and sought without success in some manner to recall his fleeing son Pepin. But while the latter was eluding him, a very harsh, rigorous winter settled. At first came torrential floods, then icy bitterness freezing the wet earth,[26] making it so perilous that even with expert horses it would be a remarkable person who would resort to such mode of travel.[27] The army therefore, becoming disheartened by an effort so great and so inconvenient, suffered repeated and dangerously unexpected attacks by the Aquitanians. The emperor decided to go to the villa called Rets and there to cross the Loire river to spend the winter in Frankland. And so he did, although less honorably than befitted him.

48:1. The devil, long hostile to the human race and to peace, was in no wise tricked by the emperor's success, but was stirring up the sons through the cunning of his accomplices, persuading them that their father wished to destroy them wantonly, not reflecting that he who was very mild to foreigners could be inhuman to his own. But, since "evil communications corrupt good manners," [28] and a gentle drop of water striking very often is wont to bore through the hardest stone,[29] it finally came to pass that they caused the emperor's sons to form a common league and muster as large an army as they could. They invoked Pope Gregory under the pretext that he alone ought and could reconcile sons to father. Afterwards, however, the truth became obvious. Later in the month of May[30] the emperor came to Worms with a strong force and there debated for a long time what should be done. Through designated emissaries, Bishop Bernard [31] and others, he urged his sons to return to him. It was asked respecting the pope of the Roman see why, if he were present after the manner of his predecessors, he contrived such great delays so as not to meet the emperor. A rumor spread abroad and confirmed what was true about the others, but it alleged that the Roman pope was present to ensnare the emperor and the bishops in the toils of excommunication if there were any disobedience to his will and that of the emperor's sons. But that audacious presumption was insufficient to steal away the emperor's bishops who declared that they would in no wise yield to his judgment. For if the pope had come to excommunicate, he would have gone away himself excommunicated, since the authority of the ancient canons held otherwise.

48:2. At length the assembly was held on the festival of John, Christ's holy forerunner,[32] at the place which—from what happened there—has been branded with a name of perpetual infamy,[33] the "Field of Lies." For those who had sworn fealty to the emperor lied, and the name of the place where that occurred has remained ever since a witness of the faithlessness. When they stood, however, with ranks arrayed not far from each other and the rush to arms was imminent, it was announced to the emperor that the Roman pope was approaching. The emperor, in battle formation, received him as he came, although less fittingly than was appropriate, charging that he who had come in such an unaccustomed manner would have prepared a similar reception for him.[34] But the pope, escorted into the field tent, pressed the emperor with oaths that he had undertaken so great a journey for no reasons other than the report that the emperor was struggling against his sons in unyielding discord [35] and the pope's desire to sow peace between both parties. The emperor's position was then stated and the pope remained with him several days before being sent back to the sons to contrive a mutual peace. Partly distracted by bribes, partly seduced by promises, partly frightened by threats, almost all the people were surging like a torrent to the sons and their followers. The pope's efforts were in vain. With as many troops brought thither and wrested from the emperor, the defection became stronger day by day, so that on the feast of Saint Paul [36] the populace, fawning upon his sons, was threatening to launch an attack on the emperor. Not able to resist those forces, the emperor ordered his sons not to expose themselves to popular pillaging. They in turn commanded him to abandon camp and come to them, asserting that they would eagerly go out to meet him. And so they did, but the emperor warned his sons, as they leaped from their horses to meet him, to remember their promise concerning himself, his son [Charles], and his wife, and to preserve unimpaired the things which they had formerly promised. Embracing them as they replied suitably, he proceeded to their camp. As he was going, his wife was led away and directed to the tents of Louis [of Bavaria]. But Lothair escorted the emperor along with Charles, then still a boy, to his own tents, and made them remain with a few men in a pavilion prepared for the purpose.

48:3. After these events the people were bound by oaths and the empire was partitioned among the brothers by a threefold division. Received by King Louis, his father's wife was again banished, this time to Italy, to the city of Tortona.[37] Observing such things, Pope Gregory returned with heavy grief to Rome. Pepin went back to Aquitaine and Louis to Bavaria. Then Lothair, taking along his father, who rode behind in a private capacity with appointed deputies, came to the villa of Marlenheim where he lingered as long as he could. Arranging such matters as appeared and satisfying the people, but appointing an assembly at Compiègne, he crossed the Vosges by way of Maurmünster and came to Mediomatricus (which is Metz by another name). He moved up to Verdun and entered the city of Soissons. There he ordered his father to be held under strict surveillance in the monastery of Saint Médard and Charles committed to Prüm but not tonsured. Lothair hunted eagerly until in the season of autumn, that is, on the Kalends of October,[38] he went to Compiègne, as had been decreed, leading his father with him.

49:1. While he was there an embassy from the emperor of Constantinople, Mark, archbishop of Ephesus and first swordsman of the emperor, accredited to his father, met him [Lothair], offered the gifts designated for him, but withheld those sent to his father. Although dispatched to his father, Lothair received the legate as though coming to him, listened to him, then dismissed him to carry back an account of this almost incredible tragedy. At the same assembly, although many were suspected of loyalty to the

father and of rebellion against the son, some tempered their
asseverations with simple words, but others with oaths.
Yet such mercy and such a change of things, with the
authors released, inspired every one. Wherefore the con-
spirators of the unheard-of crime, fearing that if things
were reversed the consequences might not be tolerable,
used an ingenious argument (so it seemed) with some of
the bishops, namely, that in addition to that for which
the emperor had already done penance, an irrevocable public penance, with arms laid aside, should again be decreed
to satisfy the church. But not even the civil laws bring
punishment twice upon one fault committed only once
and our law may not hold God to judge twice on the
very same issue.[39] A few disputed the decision, many assented, but the majority, as usual in such affairs, agreed
verbally so as not to offend the magnates. Thus adjudged,
although absent, unheard, not confessing, not tried, they
compel the emperor, before the body of Saint Médard
confessor and Saint Sebastian martyr, to lay aside his weapons and place them on the altar. Then, clothed in dark-
colored vesture, they thrust him under keep with a large
guard.

49:2. This business completed by Martinmas,[40] the people
were granted leave to go back to their own lands, full of sad-
ness for such deeds. Lothair, leading his father along, returned
to winter at Aachen. All during the winter the people of
Frankland and of Burgundy, of Aquitaine and of Germany,
assembled in throngs to express indignation at the emperor's
misfortune. Count Eggebard and Constable William[41] indeed organized against Frankland an association for the
purpose of reinstating the emperor. Abbot Hugo[42] was dispatched from Germany to Aquitaine by Louis and by those

who had fled thither, by Bishop Drogo and the rest, to arouse the interest of Pepin. Bernard and Warinus were inflaming the people in Burgundy with persuasive addresses, were enticing them with promises, were binding them with oaths, and were uniting them into one will.[43]

50. The winter passed and spring [834] presented its rosy face. Lothair—his father having been taken through the Haspengau countryside—set out and came to the city of Paris where he had commanded all his faithful to meet him. Against him advanced Count Eggebard and other nobles of that country with a great band collected to fight for the emperor's liberation. Matters would have reached that eventuality if the most pious emperor, on guard against the peril of the many as well as of his own, had not by command and adjuration prevented them from this undertaking. The assembly was finally held in the monastery of Saint Denis the martyr.

51:1. But Pepin, departing from Aquitaine with a great host and coming up to the Seine, halted there since demolished bridges and sunken boats prevented a crossing. Then Counts Warinus and Bernard, with a great many allies assembled from the regions of Burgundy, came up to the Marne. There, partly delayed by the severity and unseasonableness of the wind, partly checked to muster their allies, they settled for several days in the villa of Boneuil and those estates which lie around. The holy season of Lent[44] was at hand. In the first week, on the fifth feria, legates (Abbot Atrebaldus and Count Gautselm)[45] were sent by them to the emperor's son Lothair, demanding that the emperor be released from the bonds of confinement and handed over to them. If Lothair would heed their demand, they would place themselves at his disposal for the sake of

the dignity and honor which he formerly had from his father. If otherwise, they would seek him out, at their own
peril if need be, and with God as judge they would attack
those resisting in this matter. To the ultimatum Lothair replied reasonably that no one suffered more in his father's
calamity or rejoiced more in his father's good fortune than
he did; that the blame of priority imputed to him should not
be so attributed since they too had deserted and betrayed the
emperor; and that the mark of prison confinement was not
unlawfully imprinted upon his father since it was in accordance with an episcopal judgment. Sent forward, therefore, with this explanation, the legates returned to those
who had commissioned them.

51:2. Counts Guerinus and Odo, and Abbots Fulco and
Hugo,[46] were ordered to come to consider with him
[Lothair] how their demand could be fulfilled. The emperor's son Lothair also gave order that emissaries be dispatched tomorrow to learn the time of the approach of
the aforesaid men, so that he could meet them on the
agreed day to treat concerning the case. But the plan
was changed. Leaving his father at Saint Denis, he and
those induced by his favor repaired to Burgundy, to Vienne,
where he chose to pitch camp. The ones who had remained
with the emperor urged him to resume the imperial badges
of honor, for although he was put away from communion
with the church in the manner aforesaid, yet was he in no
wise content with that hasty decision. On the morrow, being
Sunday,[47] he sought to be reconciled by the ministry of the
bishops in the church of Saint Denis, and he agreed to be
girded with arms by the hands of the prelates. In this
matter the joy of the people increased so greatly that even
the weather, which seemed to suffer with him as he en-

dured injury, now rejoiced with him as he was relieved. For up to that time the force of tempests and violence of rains had beat so heavily that waters had flooded beyond wont and winds had rendered the channels of rivers impassable. But at his absolution the elements seem to have conspired, so that soon the raging winds became gentle and the face of the sky reverted to its ancient and long-impeded serenity.

52:1. The emperor undertook a journey from that place, but did not seek to pursue his departing son, although many were pressing him to do so. From that place therefore he went to Nanteuil and thereafter to the royal villa of Kierzy where remaining a while he awaited his son Pepin and the ones who were tarrying beyond the Marne. He waited also for those who had taken refuge beyond the Rhine with his son Louis and for that son Louis himself who was on his way to him. While he was there in the mid-season of Lent[48] (when even the joyfulness of the day itself smiled and the ecclesiastical *cantilena* of the Office [Introit] encouraged, saying: "Rejoice, Jerusalem, and all you who love her, make holy day"),[49] a great multitude of his faithful ones met him there and congratulated him with mutual rejoicing. Receiving them kindly and thanking them for the integrity of their fealty, the emperor dismissed his son Pepin to Aquitaine with joy; the others he allowed to return rejoicing to their own lands. He came, however, to Aachen, where he received Judith Augusta, Rathaldus the bishop and Boniface and Pepin bringing her back from Italy.[50] Thereafter he kept his son Charles with him for a long time. With accustomed devotion he observed the solemnity of Easter.[51] After the celebration he busied himself with hunting in the Ardennes forest. When the holy feast of Pentecost[52] had passed, he gave attention to hunting and fishing in the regions of Remiremont.

52:2. Although the emperor's son Lothair had discreetly withdrawn from his father and departed to the districts mentioned above, there still remained in the domain of Neustria Count Lantbert and Matfrid and a great many others who strove to maintain control of the areas by their own strength. Count Odo and many who favored the emperor's faction[53] tolerated that fact with impatience and gathered forces against them, endeavoring to hurl them from those places or join battle with them. This matter was managed more slowly than was fitting and was heeded less prudently and it brought upon them no little mischief. For when the enemy came upon them without warning, they, exercising less caution than occasion required, bared their backs to the foe[54] pressing upon them.

52:3. There Odo himself and his brother William, as well as a great many others, perished; still others put their safety in flight.[55] Since it did not seem sufficiently safe to remain there, and since they could not join themselves to Lothair, those who achieved the victory feared that the emperor would come upon them if they lingered or would surely meet them as they hastened to their own people. They sent therefore to Lothair as quickly as possible that he might bring them aid since they were surrounded and were apprehensive of their distance from him. Lothair determined to assist them.[56] At that season Count Warinus with a great many allies fortified the castle of Châlon so that if a revolution should be attempted by the zealous ones of the hostile parties[57] it would serve as a refuge and bulwark for himself and his men. When that had been ascertained by Lothair, he decided to advance thither, unexpectedly if possible, but it proved impossible. He did advance, however, and did invest the town, the outskirts of which were put to the torch.[58] The battle raged bitterly for five days,[59] but at last the city was captured, then (after the fashion of cruel conquerors) churches were pillaged, treasuries were robbed, and public supplies were plundered. Finally the city was given up to devouring fire, except one small basilica which by an outstanding miracle could not be burned although it was engulfed with roaring and lapping flames.[60] It had been consecrated to God under the invocation of blessed George the martyr. Yet it was not Lothair's wish for the city to be set afire. After the town was taken, Count Gotselin, Count Sanila, and Madalelm,[61] vassal of the Lord Emperor, were beheaded by a military court. Gerberga, daughter of the late Count William, was strangled by water as a witch.[62]

53:1. While these things were being done, the emperor with his son Louis had advanced to the city of the Lingones[63] where he received a messenger of these events which made him exceedingly sorrowful. His son Lothair took the road from Châlon to Autun, thence to the city of Orléans, and from there came into the country of Le Mans to a villa named *Matualis*.[64] The emperor, with great forces and with his son Louis, pursued him. When Lothair heard that, he assembled his own army and pitched camp at no great distance from his father. There was a delay of four days while legates were running back and forth. On the fourth night Lothair and all his men discreetly undertook to retreat, but the emperor his father went around by a short way until the Loire river had been reached near the fortress of Blois where the Cisse river flows into the Loire. When camps had been erected here and there, the son Pepin went

to meet his father with as great a military display as he
could muster. Subdued therefore by might, Lothair approached his father as a suppliant. When Lothair and his
chiefs had been bound by words and pledged by what
oaths were possible, the emperor sent him back to Italy,
where the narrow defiles of the roads which cross into
Italy had been stopped up so that no one might pass without permission of the garrison. The emperor then came
to Orléans with his son Louis and there granted to his son
and to the others leave to return to their own lands, after
which he advanced to Paris.

53:2. About Martinmastime[65] he held a general assembly
at the Attigny palace. There he tried unsuccessfully to
purge many things which had become notorious in ecclesiastical and public affairs. He ordered his son Pepin through
Abbot Ermold[66] to restore to the church without delay
those ecclesiastical properties in his domain which he had
allotted to his men or which they had seized for themselves.
Dispatching emissaries throughout the cities and monasteries,
he ordered to be restored to its ancient condition the
ecclesiastical organization which had almost collapsed. He
likewise enjoined that the emissaries go through each country to check the barbarism of robbers and brigands which
had arisen to incredible proportions. Where the major pirate
force was concentrated, he gave orders to impress neighboring counts and bishops' men to vanquish such folk and
crush them, and to report to him about each instance at
the next general diet at Worms,[67] which he announced
would be held when winter had passed and when the
grace of springtime made it advisable.

54:1. The emperor spent the greatest part of the winter
season at Aachen.[68] Before the Lord's Nativity (which he

observed at Metz with his brother Drogo) he set out thence
to Thionville where he celebrated the Purification of Saint
Mary[69] and whither the people came to whom the order
had been given. There he made complaint against certain
bishops involved in his ejection, some of whom had sought
asylum in Italy, others when bidden had refused to obey.
Of those who were required, Ebbo alone was present.[70]
When pressed to give a reason for his actions, he pleaded
to be questioned away from all those in whose presence
these things had been done. The other bishops insisted that
a bishop had to be present to be tried and alleged their
own innocence. At length Ebbo, offended by such matters,
sought their advice. He then announced a decision against
himself, protesting that he was unworthy of the priesthood
and sentenced himself to abstain from it. This he proclaimed
to the bishops and through them to the emperor. Afterwards Archbishop Agobard of Lyons,[71] who when ordered
to apologize postponed coming although he had been summoned three times, was removed from the leadership of the
church, while the others, as we have noted, fled to Italy.
But on the ensuing Sunday, which preceded the beginning
of holy Lent,[72] the Lord Emperor, the bishops, and all the
people of that assembly came into the city of Metz. Amid
the celebration of Masses seven archbishops intoned over
him the seven collects of ecclesiastical reconciliation. Wit-
nessing this, all the people gave thanks to God for the
emperor's plenary restoration.

54:2. Following the action, the Lord Emperor as well
as his people returned to Thionville, and when the Lord's
holy season of Lent[73] began he ordered each to return to
his own lands. He himself passed the Lenten season in that
place, but celebrated Easter in Metz.[74] After the Paschal

solemnity and the venerable day of Pentecost,[75] he departed
to the city of the Vangiones which is now called Worms[76]
to hold a general assembly according to engagement. His
son Pepin met him there and his other son Louis was also
present. As was his custom, the emperor suffered that assembly in no wise to be unoccupied with public welfare.
For in it he took pains carefully to examine what each of
the emissaries dispatched to different regions had done.
And because several of the counts were found slothful in
repressing and crushing bandits, he flayed their slothfulness
with fitting lash in appropriate expressions of his sentiment.
He admonished his sons and people to love justice, repress
robbers, and relieve from oppression all good men and their
possessions, threatening that he would hurl an even severer
judgment against those who would not conform to this
admonition.

54:3. When he had dismissed the people from this diet
and had decreed the next one at Thionville after Easter,[77]
he withdrew to winter at Aachen.[78] He commanded his son
Lothair to array all of his nobles at the same place in order
that mutual reconciliation between the emperor and Lothair
might be displayed. Since it appeared that the emperor's
body was failing and that death might not be far distant,
the emperor's counselors and Judith Augusta devised a plan
to protect her and Charles from danger: it was to win the
advocacy of one of the older brothers. Believing that none
of the emperor's sons would be as convenient for this purpose as Lothair, they urged the emperor to dispatch peace-
making emissaries to him and to invite him for this end.
Ever jealous for peace, ever the lover of peace and friend
of stability, the emperor always sought not only for his
sons but also for his enemies to be at one with him in charity.

55:1. Thereafter, in the designated villa[79] and at the appointed time,[80] the emissaries whom he had ordered were present from his son, a great many indeed, among whom Wala was the foremost. The aforesaid case having been aired and brought to a conclusion, the emperor with his wife wanted with great eagerness and kindness of heart to be reconciled first to Wala himself, remitting whatever transgressions he had committed against them. Through him and others he commanded Lothair to come as quickly as possible. If Lothair should do that, he was made to understand that it would be most advisable. They went and related the matter to the son.[81] But the emperor's desire was brought to naught, since disease and fever interposed. Wala was removed from human affairs[82] and Lothair was driven to bed, remaining listless for a very long time. But when the compassionate emperor heard that his son was afflicted with ill health, he inquired of him through loyal emissaries, through his brother Hugo and Count Adalgarius. He took pains to appreciate all of Lothair's misfortunes, imitating as it were blessed David who, although defied by his son with many abuses, nevertheless bore his death with great distress.[83]

55:2. But after Lothair had convalesced from grievous lassitude, a report came to the emperor that he was violating the conditions of oaths long ago pledged, that his men were harassing with special brutality the church of Saint Peter, which the emperor as well as his grandfather Pepin and his father Charles had undertaken to safeguard. This information so exasperated the emperor's mind, usually very mild, that in a seemingly extraordinary manner he dispatched emissaries with almost insufficient time to make so long a journey. He sent legates to Lothair, admonishing him not to permit such things to be done, warning him to remember that when the emperor assigned him the kingdom of Italy, the emperor at the same time committed to him the care of the holy Roman church, and what Lothair had sworn to defend against adversaries he should in no wise permit to be shattered by his own men. He recalled, moreover, Lothair's recent oaths to the emperor, lest by forgetting them and holding them as of small worth Lothair offend Divinity and thus incur condign punishment.[84] The emperor also ordered Lothair to have ready as tribute provisions and suitable camps along the entire way which led to Rome. For, he said, he wished to visit the thresholds of the blessed Apostles. An incursion of Northmen into Frisia prevented that from taking place. Marching to quell their daring, he sent emissaries to Lothair, namely, Abbot Fulco, Count Richard, and Abbot Atrebaldus, that Fulco and Richard might bring him a reply from Lothair, that Atrebaldus might press on directly to Rome to consult Pope Gregory on needful matters and to convey the emperor's will and other orders.[85] But Lothair, agreeing to these things, consented also respecting certain properties in Italy which had been taken away from several churches. On some matters, however, he replied that he could not save them.[86] Fulco and Richard therefore relate such things to the emperor when he returned from Frisia, after the flight of the Northmen,[87] to the palace at Frankfurt, where the emperor was then engaging in the autumn hunt before going back to winter in Aachen.[88]

56:1. But Atrebaldus went on to Rome[89] as commanded and found Lord Pope Gregory ailing with a slow but severe flow of blood from his nose. At the emperor's words and sympathy, he was refreshed with such speed and joy that he professed himself almost forgetful of his infirmity. He attended to Atrebaldus in a very sumptuous manner as long as he remained with him, and as he departed, dowered him very richly, sending two bishops with him, Peter of the city of Civitavecchia and Bishop George, regionary of the city of Rome.

56:2. When Lothair learned of the departure of the aforesaid bishops to the Lord Emperor, he sent to Bologna Leo who at that time held high post with him and who, threatening with great terror, hindered the bishops from proceeding further. But Atrebaldus secretly received a letter from them addressed to the emperor and in turn entrusted it to one of his men disguised as a beggar to carry until he might cross the Alps and reach the emperor.[90] It is lamentable to relate how at that season a great and mortal plague assailed the people who followed Lothair. For in the short interval from the Kalends of September up to Martinmas,[91] these nobles departed from this life: Jesse,[92] formerly bishop of Amiens; Helias,[93] bishop of the city of Troyes; Wala,[94] abbot of the monastery of Corbie; Matfrid, Hugo, Lambert,[95] Godefrid and his son Godefrid; Agimbert, count of Pertois; Burgaret, erstwhile prefect of the royal hunters. Richard barely escaped and not long afterwards he, too, did die.[96] These were they by whose departure Frankland was deprived of her nobility, emasculated of her strength as of nerves which had been severed, annulled of her wisdom. With these torn away, however, God shows how salutary, how praiseworthy it is to observe what is represented as proceeding from His mouth, saying: "Let not the wise man glory in his wisdom, nor the mighty man in his might, nor the rich man in his riches." [97] But who may worthily marvel at the emperor's mind, with what great self-control

divine mercy directed him? For hearing this from a messenger, he neither exulted secretly nor taunted openly because of the death of his enemies. On the contrary, beating
his breast with his fist,[98] his eyes filled with tears, he prayed
with heavy sighing for God to be propitious to them.[99] At
that time an assault of the Bretons was set in motion, but
it quieted down in such degree as the emperor placed his
trust in Him to Whom it is most truthfully said: "It is for
Thee, O Lord, to be powerful when Thou wilt." [100]

56:3. In those very days[101] also in which the Purification
of Most Blessed Mary Ever-Virgin was celebrated,[102] a
great assembly, particularly of bishops, convened at Aachen.
After other needful advantages of the church had been
disposed of, indignation was then voiced especially about
those properties which Pepin and his men had taken away
from many churches. On account of this, imperial authority
and the admonition of the general council were expressed
whereby Pepin and his men were reminded with what
great peril they violated ecclesiastical lands. This matter had
a successful termination. For Pepin, graciously receiving
the warnings of his pious father and of the holy men,
obediently complied: he decreed under the seal of his
signet-ring that all the violated lands be restored.

57. The assembly following[103] this diet the emperor held
with his sons Pepin and Louis in the regions of Lyons, in
the summer time, at a place called Crémieux.[104] The lassitude
of the aforementioned illness hindered Lothair from being
present. Here the emperor caused to be aired the case of
the vacant churches of Lyons and Vienne, since the former
bishop, Agobard, although under command, would not
come, and Bernard of Vienne, who had indeed intended to
be present, had again taken flight. This matter, of course,

remained unsettled [105] because of the absence of the bishops. But the case of the Goths was also aired there. Some of them favored Bernard's factions, others were influenced by partiality to Berengar, son of former Count Unruoch.[106] But after Berengar had been snatched away by untimely death, the greatest possible power in Septimania continued with Bernard. Legates were dispatched thither to adjust to a better condition those things which needed amendment. This having been achieved, the sons and the people having been dismissed, and the autumn hunt having been accomplished, the emperor returned at Martinmas[107] to Aachen to spend the winter. There also he celebrated the Lord's Nativity[108] and the Paschal solemnity according to the due custom always most familiar to him.[109]

58:1. But in the midst of the Paschal festivity[110] an omen (a heavenly body, a comet), foreboding and sad, appeared in the sign of Virgo, in that part of the sign where under its mantle it shackles the tail of Serpens and Corvus.[111] For twenty-five days it traveled, not toward the east after the manner of the seven wandering stars (which is marvelous to relate),[112] and passed through the signs of Leo, Cancer, and Gemini.[113] At length it fixed its fiery mass and numerous rays (which it had formerly spread in every direction) in the head of Taurus under the feet of Auriga.[114] When the emperor first observed it, he stood still, gazing. Being curious about such things he took pains, before he yielded his members to rest, to interrogate a certain man who had been sent for, that is, me,[115] who have written these things and who am credited with having knowledge of the subject. When asked about this occurrence, I requested time in which to study the form of the heavenly body, that by this means I might investigate the nature of the matter, and that I might report on the morrow what was ascertained. The emperor, supposing correctly that I wanted to "redeem the time" [116] lest it force me to reply something sorrowful, said: "Go into the enclosure adjoining this house and report to us what you have observed. For I know that this is a star not seen by me or by you on last evening. I am aware that this is a comet such as we have often spoken of in days gone by. Make known, therefore, what it seems to you to portend."

58:2. When I spoke about some things and was mute about others, he said: "There is one thing which you are still concealing in silence. For they say that by this token a change in the realm and the death of a prince are made known." Although I quoted in general the testimony of the prophet who declared, "Be not dismayed by the signs in the sky at which the nations shudder," [117] the emperor, employing his usual magnanimity and wisdom, replied: "We should fear only Him Who is the Creator of both us and that heavenly body. But we cannot praise or marvel enough at His mercy, Who vouchsafes with such disclosures to admonish our rudeness, although we are sinful and impenitent beings. Since therefore this prodigy affects both me and everyone jointly, let us all hasten to the better things conformably to our ability and discernment, lest perchance we be found unworthy of His mercy because our impenitence obstructs when He makes a preliminary offer of mercy."

58:3. Having made this statement, he indulged for a little while in unmixed wine and invited all to do the same. Then he enjoined each one to gather to his own lands. He kept that night as a vigil [118] (so we have been told) and as dawn approached offered it to God laden with praises and supplications. In the twilight of early morning he summoned his court servants and commanded that alms be distributed as generously as possible to the poor and to the servants of God, to monks and to canons. He caused solemn Masses to be celebrated by as many priests as possible,[119] not so much fearing for himself as having in mind the church entrusted to him. These matters duly disposed of as he had ordained, he set forth to the Ardennes. The hunt, they say, resulted favorably for him beyond what was usual. And everything which at that time pleased him moved quickly with good success.

59:1. In the meanwhile, the Augusta and the palatine ministers pressing vigorously, the emperor at Aix assigned a certain portion of the empire to his well-beloved son Charles, but because it remained without official proclamation,[120] it was also concealed in silence by us.[121] The other brothers were distressed when they heard about it and they entered a mutual conference.[122] Observing, however, that they could not oppose it and pretending that their gathering was for a feast, they easily allayed the agitations which seemed to have come to their father because of that. Steadfast in these things all summer, the emperor announced a general assembly at Kierzy in the autumn, that is, in the middle of September.[123] At that place and time his son Pepin came from Aquitaine with interest in that assembly. When the Lord Emperor had girded his son Charles with manly weapons, especially with a sword, and placed on his head a royal crown, he assigned him the portion of the realm which Charles's ancestor of the same name had held, namely, Neustria. Having bound the yoke of friendship between his sons as far as possible, the emperor dismissed Pepin to Aquitaine and Charles to the portion of the realm allotted to him. Those magnates of the province of Neustria

who were present gave their hands to Charles and swore
oaths of fealty; each one of the absent nobles later did the
same thing. At that place and time almost all the nobles of
Septimania were present, complaining against Bernard, duke
of those regions, because his followers were wilfully mis-
using ecclesiastical as well as private properties without regard for God or man. They begged the Lord Emperor to
take them under his protection and to dispatch emissaries
with authority and wisdom to weigh with equitable balance
concerning the stolen lands and to uphold the ancestral law.
According to their request and the Lord Emperor's choice
there were sent Count Boniface and Count Donatus as well
as Abbot Atrebaldus of the monastery of Flavigny. The
matters having been duly executed, the emperor removed
from that place and according to custom gave attention to
the autumn hunt,[124] then betook himself to Aix to pass the
winter season.[125]

59:2. When that winter had passed, on the Kalends of
January[126] the terrible fire of a comet appeared in the sign
of Scorpio not long after sunset. The death of Pepin followed soon after its menacing apparition.[127] In the meanwhile Judith Augusta, mindful of the plan which she had
initiated with the palace counselors and other nobles of the
Frankish realm, persuaded the emperor to dispatch emissaries to his son Lothair intimating to him that, if he wished
to be the guardian and helper, the protector and defender,
of his brother Charles, he should come to his father and learn
from him personally that he would obtain clemency for
everything done wrongly and would at the same time
secure half of the empire, Bavaria alone excepted.[128] To
Lothair as well as to his men this proposal seemed advantageous in every respect.

60. He came therefore to Worms, according to appointment, after the solemnity of Easter.[129] His father received him with eagerness, ordered his men to be cared for lavishly, and did all the things that he had promised. A truce of three days having been granted Lothair, the emperor agreed to divide his whole empire with them, if it was pleasing, but so that the designation of the portions would remain with the emperor and Charles. Otherwise Lothair might rather propose the partition of the empire for the emperor and Charles.[130] Lothair and his men, however, entrusted the apportionment of the realm to the Lord Emperor as he deemed proper, asserting that they could in no wise execute the division because of lack of knowledge of the places. The emperor and his men therefore divided, with equitable balance as it seemed to them, his entire empire, except Bavaria which he left to Louis and assigned to no one else. These things having been completed, and the sons and all the people having been summoned, Lothair chose his portion southward from the Meuse river, but left for his brother Charles the western part, signifying before all the people that he wished Charles to have it. While all the people applauded, the emperor heartily rejoiced and said that all things were pleasing to him. But the mind of Louis [of Bavaria] was grieved not a little. The emperor then gave thanks to God for these accomplishments and admonished his sons to be of one mind and to support each other, charging that Lothair indeed assume care of the younger brother whose spiritual father he was, and that Charles offer the honor due to a spiritual father and an elder brother. When the emperor, lover of true peace, had finished this and had sowed a mutual love between the brothers and as far as possible a reciprocal love between the adherents of each brother,

he joyfully dismissed a rejoicing Lothair to Italy enriched with many gifts, dowered with fatherly blessings, and admonished not to forget what he [Lothair] had recently promised. The emperor therefore observed the Lord's Nativity[131] and the solemnity of Easter very festively at Aix.[132]

61:1. But hearing about his father's disposition toward his brothers and about the division of the realm between them, Louis [of Bavaria] did not endure it willingly.[133] He determined to make formal demand for whatever was beyond the Rhine.[134] When this was made known to the emperor, he judged that a decision could be postponed until the Paschal feast had been completed. When that, however,[135] was finished, deeming that[136] there should be no delay in such matters, the emperor crossed the Rhine and the Main[137] and came to Tribur, where he settled for some time in order to muster his army. Then he proceeded as far as Bodman, where his son came as a reluctant suppliant. Rebuked by the emperor, Louis admitted that he had acted wickedly and he promised that he would amend the things he had done amiss. But the emperor, employing the friendly gentleness always characteristic of him, forgave his son and upbraided him, at first somewhat harshly (as was appropriate), but afterwards with softer, more caressing words. He then left him in his domain.[138]

61.2. Returning to the Rhine he crossed at the place which is called Coblenz to engage in his accustomed hunting in the Ardennes.[139] While he was busily employed in that, proven messengers arrived before him, asserting (quite truthfully) that some of the Aquitanians were awaiting his decision how the affairs of the kingdom of Aquitaine should be arranged, but some were seething with indignation because they had heard that the kingdom was given to Charles. While the emperor was disturbed about such matters, Ebroin, the noble bishop of Poitiers, came to Vlatten, reporting that he, as well as the other chiefs of the same kingdom, were awaiting the emperor's will and would obey his sovereign command. For the greatest of the magnates were in harmony with this decision; of whom outstanding ones were the same venerable Bishop Ebroin, Count Reginhard, Count Gerard (son-in-law of the late Pepin), and Count Ratharius (also a son-in-law of Pepin).[140] A great many others acquiescing in the decision could be dissuaded from it by no conspiracy. But another faction of the people, of whom the greatest was a certain Emenus, taking to themselves the son of the former King Pepin, also named Pepin, were roaming about wherever they could, as is customary with such people, devoting themselves to pillage and misrule.

61:3. The aforesaid prelate Ebroin therefore besought the emperor not to permit this disease to grow any further, but to let it be speedily remedied through his arrival before so great a plague could infect a still greater number. The emperor immediately sent the aforesaid bishop back to Aquitaine with many expressions of gratitude and with proper instructions to his loyal men. He ordered that several of them meet him in the autumn at Châlon, where he appointed a general assembly. Let no one hereafter indignantly suppose that the emperor wished cruelly to deprive his own grandson of a realm. He himself, as one reared among them, understood the native custom of those people, namely, that in order to discredit gravity and stability, pursuing inconstancy and other vices, and in order to be able to make his grandson[141] Pepin such a man, they had driven

from the frontiers of Aquitaine almost everyone who had
been sent out as guardian (as formerly guardians had been
granted to the emperor by his father Charles). After the
withdrawal of the guardians, how many and how great were
the monstrous evils and vices both public and private which
appeared in the realm, the modern inclination of contemporaries makes manifest. The most pious emperor, wishing
for the boy to be trained devoutly and with propriety,
lest prostituted by vices he might afterwards govern and
serve neither himself nor others, pondered the excuse one
man is said to have made, who was also unwilling to hand
over a realm to sons of tender age: "Not because I envy those
born of me do I forbid them to hold places of honor, but
because I know that those dignities add fuel to ferocity in
youths." [142] The emperor therefore, as he had appointed,
came to the city of Châlon in the autumn[143] and disposed in
his usual fashion affairs of the church as well as of the
state, then addressed himself to the succession of the kingdom of Aquitaine. With the queen, his son Charles, and a
strong force he removed from Châlon and crossing the
Loire sought out the city of Auvergne. There, in a kindly
manner according to due custom, he received the loyal ones
who came to meet him and caused them to commend themselves to his son Charles by the usual oaths. Certain ones,
however, came to the obligatory meeting and swore fealty,
then prowled about the army to plunder and carry off
whatever spoils they could. He gave orders to arrest them
and put them to the legal question.

62:1. Having done these things he celebrated the Lord's
Nativity festival at Poitiers with due and customary honor.[144]
While he was lingering there and adjudicating whatever
public welfare required,[145] a messenger came, saying that

his son Louis had invaded Alamannia with some Saxons and
Thuringians. This matter constituted a very great misfortune
for him. For in addition to being already burdened with
old age, with his lung vexed more than usual with abundance of phlegm (which increased in winter) and with his
chest disturbed, to him in such condition this sorrowful
messenger also chanced to come. Although in nature the
emperor was very mild (almost beyond human measure), in
resolution magnanimous, in piety most circumspect, he was
so bitterly weakened by the report that the increasing mucus
hardened into an abscess, and a deadly ulcer began to grow
larger within his vitals. Although he learned that God's
church was being thrown into confusion and Christian
people harassed by so great a bane, his unvanquished spirit
did not yield to loathing or, shattered to pieces, succumb to
grief. Hardly had he with his wife and son Charles[146] begun
the holy fast of Lent[147] when he raised himself as a barrier to
thwart this calamity. He who had been wont with profoundest devotion to spend the entire solemn season in the singing
of Psalms, urgent prayers, celebration of Masses, and largesse
of alms, so that he scarcely conceded one or two days to
riding for exercise, now for the sake of avoiding discord
and of restoring peace, wished to have no day idle. Following the example of the Good Shepherd [148] he did not refrain
from incurring damage to his own body for the advantage of
the flock entrusted to him. There should be no doubt that
he received the reward which the All Highest and Prince of
shepherds[149] has promised to give those who labor.

62:2. With very great fatigue and with the aforesaid ailments assailing his health, he came to Aachen as the most
holy Paschal solemnity[150] drew near and there observed it
with accustomed devotion. He then hastened to complete the

business undertaken. Crossing the Rhine, he penetrated Thuringia by forced march,[151] where he had learned that Louis was lingering. Since Louis's conscience would not suffer him to delay there longer seeing that his father was already at hand, he despaired of the effort and trusted to flight for safety. Obtaining passage he returned to his lands through the country of the Slavs. In the meanwhile the emperor ordered a general assembly to be gathered in the city of the Vangiones which is now called Worms. And since the affairs of Louis were thus in abeyance, his son Charles was returned with his mother to Aquitaine.[152] The emperor sent to his son Lothair in Italy, requiring him to take part in the assembly to deliberate with him and others about this matter.

62:3. At that time, on the third day of the Major Litany,[153] a failure of the sun occurred in a preternatural manner. For at the sun's withdrawal, darkness prevailed to such an extent that nothing seemed to differ from true night. The fixed order of stars was perceived as though none of the heavenly bodies suffered from the vigor of sunlight. The moon, which had appeared over against the sun, moved little by little eastward, first restoring light to the sun on the western part like a horned crescent, according to its own fashion when the first or second phase is observed, and thus by growth the entire wheel of the sun again received its full beauty.[154] Although this prodigy is attributable to nature, it was brought to completion with lamentable result. For it presaged that the great light of mortals which shone for all, a lampstand placed in God's house above (I refer to the emperor of most pious memory), would be very swiftly taken from human affairs and that the world would be left in darkness of tribulation at his departure.

62:4. He soon thereafter began to waste away with nausea and to receive food and drink with vomiting stomach, to be oppressed with wracking sighs, to shake with choking rattles,[155] and thus to fail in strength. For when nature is deserted by its mainstays it is obvious that it is exhausted and vanquished. Perceiving this he ordered summer campaign tents to be set up for him on an island near the city of Mainz,[156] where abandoned by his powers he committed himself to his bed.

63:1. Who may unfold the emperor's apprehension for the condition of the church or his grief for its agitation? Who is there to recount the flood of tears which he shed for the hastening of divine mercy? For he grieved not that he was to depart, but what he knew would come to pass, saying that he was wretched whose last days would close with such woes. There came to comfort him venerable prelates and many other servants of God, among whom were Hethi,[157] revered bishop of Trèves; Otgar,[158] archbishop of Mainz; and Drogo, brother of the Lord Emperor, bishop of Metz, and archchaplain of the sacred palace. As near to him as the emperor knew that Drogo was, so much the more intimately he entrusted himself and all his possessions to Drogo. Through the same Drogo the emperor performed the duty of confession, "the sacrifice of a troubled spirit and a humbled heart," [159] which God does not despise. Throughout forty days the emperor's only food was the Lord's Body, as he praised the justice of God, saying: "Just art Thou, O Lord,[160] since in the past I have not spent the season of Lent in fasting, I am now compelled to keep the same fast to Thee."

63:2. He ordered that his venerable brother Drogo cause the ministers of his chamber to come before him and that he bid the household properties, the royal equipment to be described one by one, that is, crowns, arms, vessels, books, and clerical garments. The emperor gave instruction to Drogo, as seemed proper, what should be distributed to churches, to the poor, and lastly to his sons Lothair and Charles. He assigned to Lothair indeed a crown, and a sword encrusted with gold and gems, to be held on condition that he keep faith with Charles and Judith and that Lothair accord to Charles, and maintain, the full portion of the realm which, God and the nobles of the palace being witness, the emperor had bestowed upon Charles at the same time with Lothair and in his presence. When these matters had been duly accomplished, he gave thanks to God because he knew that nothing now remained his own.

63:3. During this transaction the venerable prelate Drogo and the other bishops were offering thanks[161] to God that they should be edified by seeing him, whom the choir of virtues had always attended,[162] now pursuing them steadfastly to the end like the tail of an animal and rendering all of his life "a sacrifice utterly acceptable to God." [163] Yet their joy was darkened by his last will and testament. For fearing that he might choose to remain unreconciled to his son Louis, they know that a wound often cut open or burned by cautery might generate a harsher pain for the one sustaining it. Relying nevertheless upon the unconquered patience which he always exercised, they kept playing gently on his mind through his brother Drogo, whose words the emperor was unwilling to spurn. At first he did display bitterness of mind. Considering for a while he tried, with what little breath was left, to speak of how many great inconveniences he had suffered from Louis and of what Louis should deserve for doing such things against nature and God's precept. "But," he said, "since he cannot come to me to make satisfaction, I now perform the satisfaction which is mine, with you and God as witnesses. I forgive him everything wherein he has sinned against me. It will be your duty to advise him that, if I have forgiven him things so often done wrongly, he may not forget that he was the one who led his father's grey hairs to death with sorrow and in such matters despised the precepts and warnings of God our common Father."

64:1. When these things had been done and said (it was on the evening of the sabbath),[164] he ordered that the nocturnal vigils[165] be celebrated before him and that his breast be fortified [166] by the sign[167] of the holy cross. As long as he was able, he repeatedly with his own hand sealed his forehead and breast with that sign. But when he became weary he asked with a nod that it be done by the hands of his brother Drogo. He remained therefore all that night stripped of bodily strength, possessed only of a rational mind. On the morrow, which was Sunday,[168] he commanded the mystery of the altar to be made ready and the solemnities of Mass to be celebrated by Drogo. He also ordered that Holy Communion be given to him by Drogo's hands according to custom, and that after this a little swallow of tepid drink be offered him. Sipping this he prayed his brother and those standing about to give attention to care of their bodies, that as long as he lingered so long should they be refreshed.

64:2. The moment of his departure being imminent, joining thumb with fingers (he had been accustomed to do this when he was summoning his brother with a nod), he called for his brother. Drogo approached with the other priests. The emperor, commending himself with what words he could and with nods, asked to be blessed and requested those things to be done which are wont to be done at the departure of a soul.[169] As they did that, so many have related to me, he turned his eyes to the left side, as if offended, and with as much strength as he could muster he exclaimed twice, "Hutz! Hutz!" (which signified, "Avaunt!").[170] It is obvious that he saw a malign spirit whose fellowship he, living or dying, did not want to share. But with eyes lifted heavenward, the more threateningly he gazed hither, the more joyfully he strained thither, so that he seemed to differ not a whit from one laughing.[171] In such manner therefore he obtained the end of the present life and went away to rest happily, so we believe, because, as it has been said truthfully by a truth-speaking teacher: "He cannot die badly who has lived well." [172]

64:3. He departed on the twelfth day before the Kalends of July[173] in the sixty-fourth year of his life. He presided over Aquitaine throughout thirty-seven years, but he was emperor twenty-seven.[174] His soul having withdrawn, Drogo, his brother and bishop of Metz, with the other bishops, abbots, counts, royal vassals, and a great throng of clergy and people took up the emperor's remains and caused them to be transferred with high honor to Metz and interred in a noble manner in the basilica of Saint Arnulf, where his mother was also buried.

*   *   *

The life and acts of the glorious prince,
the unconquered and orthodox emperor,
Louis the Pious,
are finished.[175]

Notes

INTRODUCTION

1. See ch. 64:3 below.
2. Ch. 56:2 and Part III, note 96.
3. Prologue (3).
4. Ch. 58:1, 58:2.
5. Prologue (1), ch. 52:1, 64:2, and elsewhere.
6. Ch. 62:1.
7. Ch. 33.
8. Chs. 21:1, 24:1, and elsewhere, M. Manitius, *Geschichte der lateinischen Literatur des Mittelalters*, I (Munich: Beck, 1911), 656, thinks he was an Aquitanian; Bernhard Simson, *Jahrbücher des fränkischen Reichs unter Ludwig dem Frommen*, II (Leipzig: Duncker und Humbolt, 1876), 297, n. 7, suggests that he was a German.
9. Prologue (3).
10. Ch. 58:1, 58:2.
11. Based on ch. 58:1, the author's reference to himself as one credited with knowledge of astronomy.
12. Chs. 27, 41:1, 58:1, 59:2, 62:3.
13. Ch. 58:1, 58:2.
14. Also observed by Wilhelm Nickel, *Untersuchungen über die Quellen, den Wert und den Verfasser der Vita Hludovici des "Astronomus"* (Potsdam: Edmund Stein, 1919), 46; and Simson, *op. cit.*, II, 295.

15. Chs. 20:3, 62:1, 62:2, 62:4, 64:2.

16. Ch. 28:1.   17. Chs. 55:1, 55:2, 57:1.

18. Ch. 56:1.   19. Chs. 44:1, 56:2, 61:3.

20. E.g., chs. 23:3, 25:1, 25:3, 30:1, 32:1, 33:1, 38:1, 45:2, 46:2, 51:1, 54:1.

21. Ch. 49:1. What the author means by *our law* is ambiguous, but it is not compellingly necessary to assume that he intends the canon law, although the language may mean that.

22. Chs. 37:2, 43:1, 50:1, 51:1.   23. Chs. 47:2, 52:1.

24. Chs. 10, 13–17, 35, 40:2, 41:1, 42:2, 42:3, 45:2, 48:2, 51:1, 52:2, 53:1, 55:2, 61:1.

25. This is the judgment of Nickel, *op. cit.*, 42, and of G. H. Pertz in his edition of the *Vita* in MGH: Scriptures, II (Hannover: Hahn, 1829), 604f.

26. Chs. 3:1, 36.   27. Chs. 6:2, 53:1, 59:1, 60.

28. Chs. 44:1, 63:3.   29. Prologue (2), chs. 56:2, 63:1.

30. Chs. 40:1, 45.   31. Ch. 45.

32. Chs. 15:2, 19:2, 58:1, 58:2.

33. Chs. 26:2, 28:1, 28:3.

34. Chs. 4:2, 8, 15:2, 50, 51:2, 52:1.

35. See below in this Introduction.

36. This is evident throughout the book, but the Prologue may be instanced here.

37. See the next section of this Introduction.

38. Ch. 19:1.

39. *Ibid.* Cf. *Chanson de Roland,* lines 1881f.: "deit monies estre en un de cez mostiers/si preierat toz jorz por noz pecchiez."

40. Ch. 27.   41. Ch. 28:3.

42. Ch. 48:1   43. Ch. 49:1.

44. With but few exceptions, these are my discovery.

45. Chs. 3, 4:1 (*bis*), 20:1, 62:1, 63:1.

46. Prologue (2), chs. 19:2, 46:1, 55:1, 56:2, 58:1, 62:1, 63:1, 63:2.

47. Prologue (2).

48. Prologue (2), chs. 40:2, 48:1.

49. Chs. 20:3, 56:2 (*bis*), 58:2.

50. Prologue (2).

51. Ch. 52:1. See H. Leclercg, "Cantilène," *Dictionnaire d'archéologie chrétienne et de liturgie*, II, Part 2 (Paris: Letouzey et Ané, 1925), 1969–75.

52. Prologue (2), chs. 40:2, 48:1. The last, I Cor. 15:33, an iambic trimeter, is from Menander's *Thais*.

53. Prologue (2), chs. 20:3, 52:1, 56:2 (*bis*), 58:2.

54. See note 45 above.

55. Prologue (2), chs. 19:2, 56:2, 58:1, 62:1.

56. I.e., Prologue (2), chs. 19:2, 62:1.

57. Most of the Biblical citations are my discovery.

58. See the following section of this Introduction.

59. The most significant attempts to suggest identification are Nickel, *op. cit.*, 44–52, and M. Buchner, "Entstehungszeit und Verfasser der 'Vita Hludowici' des 'Astronomen,'" *Historisches Jahrbuch*, LX (1940), 14–45. For lists of court-personnel, see Simson, *op. cit.*, II, 232–63.

60. The Charlemagne biography is Einhard, *Vita Karoli imperatoris*, ed. G. H. Pertz, G. Waitz, O. Holder-Egger (6th ed.; Hannover: Hahn, 1911; reprinted 1947), in the series, "Scriptores rerum Germanicarum in usum scholarum ex 'Monumentis Germaniae Historicis' separatim editi." The biographies of Louis the Pious are (1) the anonymous *Vita Hludovici pii* (here translated) in *Monumenta Germaniae Historica* [abbreviated as MGH]: Scriptores, II (Hannover: Hahn, 1829), 604–48 (text, 607–48), ed. G. H. Pertz; and in J. P. Migne, *Patrologiae cursus completus . . .: series Latina* [abbreviated as MPL], civ (Paris: Migne, 1864), 927c–78d; (2) the four books of elegiacs on the deeds of Louis the Pious by Ermoldus Nigellus in *Ermold le Noir, Poème sur Louis le Pieux et Épitres au Roi Pépin*, ed. and trans. Edmond Faral (Paris: Champion, 1932); (3) Thegan, *Vita Ludovici imperatoris* (together with a brief

continuation), ed. Pertz in MGH and reprinted in MPL, cvi, 405d–30b; and (4) Book I of Nithard's four books, *De dissensionibus filiorum Ludovici pii* in Nithard, *Histoire des fils de Louis le Pieux*, ed. and trans. Ph. Lauer (Paris: Champion, 1926).

61. Walafrid Strabo, *Visio Wettini*, 447–62 (MPL, cxiv, 1073ab); *Visio cuiusdam pauperculae mulieris*, in H. Löwe, *Die Karolinger vom Tode Karls des Grossen bis zum Vertrag von Verdun* (Weimar: Hermann Böhlaus Nachfolger, 1957), 317f., n. 85.

62. Agobard, *De dispensatione ecclesiasticarum rerum*, 3 (MPL, civ, 228b): "Hanc igitur rem cum miris tunc laudibus adhuc inchoatam magistri nostri efferrent, et praecipue venerandus senex Adalardus, qui etiam dicebat se numquam sublimius vel gloriosius causam profectus publici moveri et cogitari vidisse a tempore regis Pippini usque ad diem illum. . . ."

63. The Oxford University Press in one of its earlier announcements of the series, "Medieval Classics."

64. Prologue (2).   65. Ch. 7.

66. Ch. 56:2.   67. Chs. 33, 42:1, 45, 46:1.

68. Chs. 44:2, 62:1.   69. Ch. 24:2.

70. Ch. 18:1.   71. Ch. 21:2.

72. Ch. 23:1.   73. Ch. 21:2.

74. Ch. 48:2.   75. Ch. 63:3.

76. Ch. 10.   77. Ch. 14:2.

78. Ch. 13:1.   79. Ch. 18:2.

80. Ch. 61:3.   81. Chs. 29:2, 30:1.

82. Ch. 35:1.   83. Ch. 20:1.

84. *Ibid.*   85. *Ibid.*

86. Ch. 55:2.   87. Ch. 58:2.

88. Ch. 61:3.

89. F. L. Ganshof, "Louis the Pious Reconsidered," *History*, XLII, No. 146 (Oct. 1957), 173 and n. 5. In our contemporary parlance, however, we might interpret this as indicating that Louis was a "good executive."

90. See chs. 36, 49, 54, 63.

91. Esp. in chs. 63, 64.

92. Helen Waddell, *The Wandering Scholars* (reprinted; Garden City, N.Y.: Doubleday and Co., 1955), 50. On Louis's personality and epithets, see Simson, *op. cit.*, I, 33–46.

93. Ch. 8.   94. See Part I, note 50, below.

95. Ch. 32:2.

96. For favorable comments, see the saccharine verses of Walafrid Strabo addressed to the empress (MPL, cxiv, 1093d–94c, 1095cd, 1097b); for unfavorable, the remarks of Paschasius Radbertus later in this Introduction. Incidentally, Roland Mushat Frye, "The Teachings of Classical Puritanism on Conjugal Love," *Studies in the Renaissance*, II (1955), 148–59, should dispel any erroneous notions about Puritans and love.

97. Thegan, *op. cit.*, 19.

98. H. Graetz, *History of the Jews* (Eng. version reprinted; Philadelphia: Jewish Publication Society, 1946), III, 163.

99. This paragraph and the two preceding ones are summarized from Allen Cabaniss, "Bodo-Eleazar: A Famous Jewish Convert," *Jewish Quarterly Review*, n.s., XLIII, No. 4 (April 1953), 313–28, where full documentation is given.

100. Paschasius Radbertus, *De vita Walae seu epitaphium Arsenii*, II, 7 (MPL, cxx, 1616c).

101. Ch. 44:1.   102. Ch. 52:3.

103. Ch. 64:2.

104. Simson, *op. cit.*, II, 300 and n. 11, citing Leibniz, *Ann. Imp.*, I, 220. It is interesting, however, to observe how heavily Simson relies on this anonymous *Vita*.

105. Manitius, *op. cit.*, I, 656.

106. Cf. Arthur Winckler, *Die Krönung Karl's des Grossen zum Römischen Kaiser* (Berlin: Habel, 1879).

107. Cf. August Schmidt, *Die Sachsenkriege unter Karl dem Grossen* (Rostock: Boldt, 1882); Hermann Witzschel, *Der*

Ausgang der Sachsenkriege Karls des Grossen 792–804 (Halle: Kaemmerer, 1891).

108. M. L. W. Laistner, *Thought and Letters in Western Europe*, A.D. *500 to 900* (new ed.; Ithaca, N.Y.: Cornell University Press, 1957), 276.

109. Prologue (3).

110. Chaim Tykocinski, *Quellenkritische Beiträge zur Geschichte Ludwig des Frommen* (Leipzig: Schmidt, 1898).

111. Gerold Meyer (von Knonau), *Ueber Nithards vier Bücher Geschichten* (Leipzig: Hirzel, 1866), esp. pp. 14–18, 135f.

112. *Ibid.*

113. Nickel, *op. cit., passim* (see note 14 above).

114. *Ibid.*   115. *Ibid.*, 11–13.

116. Simson, *op. cit.*, II, 299 and n. 5. (Of course, we also know about the last detail from Einhard himself.)

117. Ch. 4:2.   118. Ch. 15.

119. Ch. 58.   120. Ch. 62:3.

121. E.g., Tacitus, *Germania*, 14.

122. Ch. 29:1.   123. Ch. 35:2.

124. Ch. 28:1.   125. Ch. 29:1.

126. Ch. 32:3.   127. Ch. 28:3.

128. Ch. 20:1.   129. Ch. 33.

130. Ch. 46:2.   131. Ch. 4:1.

132. Ch. 6:1.   133. Ch. 59:1.

134. Ch. 46:2.   135. Ch. 46:1.

136. Ch. 59:1.   137. Ch. 5.

138. *Ibid.*   139. *Ibid.*

140. Ch. 6:2.   141. Ch. 46.

142. Ch. 44:1. For remarks on court etiquette, see Simson, *op. cit.*, II, 263–65.

143. Ch. 44:2.   144. Ch. 58.

145. Ch. 21:1.   146. Ch. 24:1.

147. Ch. 59:1.   148. Ch. 26:2, 26:3.

PROLOGUE

1. "qui relatione sua." Clearly *written* narratives; see note 13 below.

2. "iter triverit." Cf. Vergil, *Georgics*, I, 380: "formica terens iter." See M. Manitius, "Zu dem Epos 'Karolus Magnus et Leo Papa,'" *Neues Archiv der Gesellschaft für ältere deutsche Geschichtskunde*, IX (1884), 618.

3. The reader will be familiar with a number of such instances.

4. This phrase could well serve as a title of the work.

5. "quia succumbit cuiusque non dico meum quod perexiguum est sed magnorum ingenium materiae tantae." Cf. Einhard, *Vita Karoli, praef.*: "cui scribendae atque explicandae non meum ingeniolum quod exile et parvum immo poene nullum est sed Tullianam par erat desudare facundiam." See M. Manitius, "Zu deutschen Geschichtsquellen des 9. bis 12. Jahrhunderts," *Neues Archiv* [see note 2 above], XI (1886), 72.

6. Wisd. 8:7. The Vulgate has *utilius* instead of *dulcius*. The four Cardinal Virtues are themes frequently discussed by pagan moralists, but our author chose to cite the Scriptural listing.

7. A Greek proverb, of course, but probably derived here from Terence, *Andria*, 61, or from St. Jerome, *Epistolae*, cviii, 20, more probably from Terence. Cf. Paschasius Radbertus, *De vita Walae seu epitaphium Arsenii*, I, 2, *ad fin.*: "Acriter invehis, frater Severe. Velim caveas illud Terrentii: 'Ne quid nimis. . . .'" See Manitius, *Geschichte*, I, 657.

8. Job 28:28.

9. Cf. Mark 12:30f and parallels; reminiscent of St. Ambrose, *De officiis ministrorum*, and therefore of Cicero, *De officiis*.

10. "uni . . . culpae succubuisse." Cf. Vergil, *Aeneid*, IV, 19: "Huic uni forsan potui succumbere culpae." See Manitius, "Zu dem Epos," 618.

11. Cf. II Cor. 12:13; the Vulgate has *donate mihi* instead of *dimitte illi*.

12. "usque ad tempora imperii." Ambiguous, suggesting either the year 800, the date of the restoration of the empire in the West, or 814, the date of Louis's accession, more likely the latter.

13. "relatione." Oral or written? Probably a *written* narrative; see note 1 above.

14. Only four details are here presented about this mysterious person: (a) he was "most noble," i.e., of noble lineage; (b) he became a monk; (c) he was of approximately the same age as Louis the Pious, i.e., born about 778; and (d) he was reared with Louis, as was also Ebbo, later the archbishop of Rheims (816–35). He may or may not be identified with the Adhemar mentioned in ch. 12 (as Louis's legate to Emperor Charles in 800), in ch. 13:2. (as standard-bearer at the siege of Barcelona on 804), in ch. 14:1 (as leader in the campaign against Tortosa in 809), and in ch. 15:1 (as leader in a similar campaign against Tortosa in 810). Cf. Nickel, *Untersuchungen*, 2–6, and Buchner, "Entstehungszeit."

15. "quia ego rebus interfui palatinis quae vidi et comperire potui stylo contradidi." Cf. Einhard, *op. cit., praef.*: "me scribere posse quibus ipse interfui quaeque praesens oculata ut dicunt fide cognovi." Despite the obvious reminiscence of Einhard's language and despite the failure to mention other known sources of his information, our author gives adequate evidence of the truth of his assertion; see especially chs. 56, 58, 64:2 below for evidence of matters reported to him by intimates of the court, and chs. 58, 59 for matters observed by him. It is clear enough, of course, that he used Einhard's *Vita Karoli*; and in chs. 21–43, the *Annales regni Francorum*. At many points in

chs. 44 to end of his work, he may have had access to the sources of the *Annales Bertiniani* and other annals, although this cannot be certainly established; see various notes below which direct attention to the similarities, and Manitius, "Zu deutschen Geschichtsquellen," 72.

PART I

1. "famosissimus regum." Cf. Einhard, *Vita Karoli, praef.*: "et merito famosissimi regis." See Manitius, "Zu deutschen Geschichtsquellen," 72.

2. *Annales regni Francorum, anno* 769; cf. Einhard, *op. cit.*, 3.

3. *Ibid., anno* 771. Carloman died on 8 Dec.; his magnates (among them Warinus and Adalard) submitted to Charles—cf. Einhard, *op. cit.*, 3.

4. *Ibid., anno* 769. Hunold had retired, but now came out of retirement; cf. Einhard, *op. cit.*, 5.

5. According to Einhard, *op. cit.*, 18–20 (and the notes by Pertz and Waitz), Charles had four wives: (1) the daughter of Desiderius, king of the Lombards, whom he married in 770 and repudiated a year later; (2) Hildigard, a noble Swabian (really an Alamannian), died 783; (3) Fastrada, an East Frank, d. 794; (4) Liutgard, an Alamannian, d. 800; and possibly six concubines: (a) Himiltrudis, (b) Sigradane (?), (c) Madelgard, (d) Gersuind, (e) Regina, and (f) Adallindis. Children were born of all except Nos. 1 and 4. Charles (d. 811), Pepin (d. 810), and Louis (the Pious) were the sons, and Hruotrud (d. 810), Bertha, and Gisla, the daughters, of Hildigard. Fastrada had two daughters, Theoderada and Hiltrud. Children of the concubines were Pepin (the Hunchback, Charles's first-born; d. 811), son of Himiltrudis; Hruodhaidis, daughter of Sigradane (?); Ruothildis, daughter of Madelgard; Adaltrud, daughter of Gersuind; Drogo (d. 855) and Hugo (d. 844), sons of Regina; and Theodoric, son of Adallindis. So Einhard and his editors. Other sources observe that Pepin, son of Hildigard, was originally

named Carloman (perhaps for Charles the Great's brother who died in 771; it is worth noting that Charles already had a son Pepin) and that another son, Lothair (twin of Louis the Pious) was born to Hildigard, but died shortly after birth. On this, see the documentation in E. S. Duckett, *Alcuin, Friend of Charlemagne* (New York: Macmillan, 1951), 92, 96; M. E. McKinney, *The Saxon Poet's Life of Charles the Great* (New York: Pageant Press, 1956), 110.

6. "reginam . . . gemina gravidam prole." Cf. Vergil, *Aeneid*, I, 274: "Marte gravis geminam partu dabit Ilia prolem." See Manitius, "Zu dem Epos," 618.

7. "quam regionem iamdudum [i.e., in 769] in deditionem susceperat Lupo principe se et sua eius nutui dedente." Cf. Einhard, *op. cit.*, 5: "Sed Lupus . . . etiam se ipsum cum provincia cui praeerat eius potestati permisit." See also *Annales regni Francorum, anno* 769, and Manitius, "Zu deutschen Geschichtsquellen," 72.

8. "superata difficultate." Cf. Einhard, *op. cit.*, 9: "saltuque Pyrenei superato"; *Annales regni Francorum, anno* 778: "superatoque . . . Pyrenei iugo"; Ammianus Marcellinus, *Rerum gestarum libri*, XIV, 2, 9: "superatis difficultatibus." See Manitius, "Zu deutschen Geschichtsquellen," 70; Nickel, *Untersuchungen*, 45.

9. "qui mons cum altitudine coelum pertingat, asperitate cautium horreat, opacitate silvarum tenebrescat." Cf. Einhard, *op. cit.*, 6: "quantoque Francorum labore invia montium iuga et eminentes in caelum scopuli atque asperae cautes superatae sint." *Ibid.*, 9: "est enim locus opacitate silvarum . . . opportunus." See Manitius, "Zu deutschen Geschichtsquellen," 72.

10. "angustia viae . . . commeatum non modo tanto exercitui . . . intercludat." Cf. Caesar, *Bellum Gallicum*, III, 23: "commeatibus nostros intercludere constituunt." See Manitius, "Zu deutschen Geschichtsquellen," 70.

11. "prospero emensus est itinere." Cf. Vergil, *Aeneid*, XI, 244: "Atque iter emensi." See Manitius, "Zu dem Epos," 618.

12. For Hannibal, see Livy, *Historiarum libri*, XXI, 23.

13. The event later celebrated as "the battle of Roncesvalles," which occurred on Saturday, 15 August 778.

14. "quorum quia vulgata sunt nomina." This indeed may or may not allude to Einhard, *op. cit.*, 9, where among the fallen heroes two or three are specifically mentioned: Eggihardus, provost of the royal table; Anshelmus, count of the palace; and Hruodlandus, prefect of the Breton frontier (in some MSS the last name does not appear). It is only just, however, to observe that our author's statement seems to imply reliance upon an oral rather than a literary tradition. Cf. Simson, *op. cit.*, II, 301. A bibliography of the Roland-legend may be derived from Leon Gautier, *Bibliographie des chansons de geste* (Paris: Welter, 1897); Joseph Bédier, *Les legendes épiques*, III (Paris: Champion, 1929); Robert Fawtier, *Le chanson de Roland: étude historique* (Paris: Boccard, 1933); Mario Pei, *French Precursors of the Chanson de Roland* (New York: Columbia University Press, 1948).

15. This twin was the Lothair mentioned in note 5 above, who died shortly after baptism "in periculo mortis."

16. Note the play on words which can, fortunately, be conveyed in translation: "Nati sunt . . . sed eum . . . renasci contigisset. . . ."

17. This is the first of three very precise dates given in this *Vita*. The other two are (1) 28 Jan. 814, date of Charles's death, ch. 20:3, and (2) 20 June [840], date of Louis's death, ch. 64.3.

18. Ermoldus Nigellus, *De rebus gestis Ludovici*, I, 49, declares that the name is derived from *hluto* ("celebrated") and *wigch* ("war" or "warrior"). Both infants, Louis and the dying Lothair, were hurriedly baptized "in periculo mortis."

19. Cf. Isa. 11:2; two of the "seven gifts" of the Holy Spirit.

20. On this word, consult C. E. Odegaard, *Vassi and Fideles in the Carolingian Empire*, Harvard Historical Monographs XIX (Cambridge: Harvard University Press, 1945), 14–50.

21. See note 19 above.

22. (Puy-en-) Vélay, on Mont Cévenne, the peak of which is in Puy en Auvergne.

23. Note the Beowulfian name.

24. A significant awareness that Rome was no longer "mistress of the world."

25. St. Peter.   26. St. Paul.

27. Cf. Matt. 28:18.

28. Pope Hadrian I, 1 Feb. 772—25 Dec. 795, a member of the noble Roman house of Colonna.

29. Apparently as chief guardian of the young king.

30. Reminiscent of I Cor. 14:40, but there is no verbal agreement.

31. "quibus difficulter expeditur aetas semel imbuta." Subtly and humorously reminiscent of Horace, *Epistolae*, I, 2, 69: "quo semel est imbuta recens servabit odorem/testa diu." See Manitius, *Geschichte*, I, 657.

32. "caligulis." One inevitably recalls the Roman emperor, Gaius, who was nicknamed Caligula.

33. See ch. 3 above.

34. "Mors-Gothorum" (Goths'-Death); perhaps Mourgoudou (dép. Tarn).

35. The later St. William of Gellone, father of Bernard of Barcelona, Heribert, and Gerberga, all mentioned below. Cf. ch. 13:2, where he is noted as the first at the siege of Barcelona, and ch. 52:3, where he is referred to as the "late count." He was of royal blood, being grandson of Charles Martel and hence first cousin of Charles the Great. On his legendary history, see Joseph Bédier, *Les legendes épiques*, I: *Le cycle de Guillaume d'Orange* (Paris: Champion, 1926).

36. "At Toulouse" omitted in some MSS.   37. Abu Taher.

38. "ense . . . accinctus est." Cf. Vergil, *Aeneid*, VII, 640: "fidoque accingitur ense." See Manitius, "Zu dem Epos," 618.

39. At Chuneberg. On Charles's wives, see note 5 above.

40. Son of Hildigard; see note 5 above.

41. "per montis Cinisii asperos et flexuosos anfractus." Cf. Ammianus Marcellinus, *op. cit.*, XVII, 1, 9: "per anfractus longos et asperos." See Manitius, "Zu deutschen Geschichtsquellen," 70.

42. The hunchback, son of Himiltrudis; see note 5 above.

43. That is, Guilbert or Gilbert, bishop of Rouen from ca. 800 until his death in 828.

44. Is this perchance the same person as the *ostiarius*, Count Richard, of chs. 55 and 56, and the *perfidus* of Thegan, *Vita Ludovici imperatoris*, appendix, who died in Nov. 842? On his death, see J. F. Böhmer, E. Mühlbacher, J. Lechner, *Die Regesten des Kaiserreichs unter den Karolingern 751–918* (Innsbruck: Verlag der Wagner'schen Universitäts-Buchhandlung, 1908), #1094. I have consulted *Die Regesten* frequently in this study. In general it relies on this *Vita* except in the tangled chronology of chs. 54–56. Most of the dates I have adapted from *Die Regesten* with no documentation apart from this general remark.

45. "misericordiae quae illi genuina probatur." A periphrasis for "his mercy."

46. "annonas militares quae vulgo foderum vocant."

47. Cf. ch. 29:2 below for reference to his son Reginherius, a former count of the imperial palace, but in 817 a traitor, whose bitter death in 818 is recorded in ch. 30:1 below.

48. Latin, Hadefonsus; prince of Asturias and Galicia, according to *Annales regni Francorum, anno* 797.

49. "et dona ferentes." Cf. Vergil, *Aeneid*, ii, 49: "et dona ferentis." It is strange that Manitius, Nickel, and others have overlooked this simple and very obvious allusion.

50. A curious remark about the "pious" Louis, the implications of which are very important. It gives weight to the probability that the shadowy child, Elpheid or Alpaïs, was indeed a daughter of Louis, his first-born, albeit illegitimate. She was married to Bigo (Bego, Biego), a dear, long-time friend of Louis, formerly his royal chamberlain and (from 814 until his death in 816) the count of Paris. See *Annales Hildesheimenses*, anno 817; Ermoldus Nigellus, *op. cit.*, I, 179–88, 274; II, 495–98. Heinrich Fichtenau, *Das karolingische Imperium* (Zürich: Fretz und Wasmuth, 1949), 316, n. 26, cites M. Chaume, *Les origines du duché de Bourgogne*, I (Dijon: Jobard, 1925), 126, n. 10, against this identification: Fichtenau states that Bigo married Alpaïs, a daughter of Charles the Great and Himiltrudis (see also *ibid.*, 125). On pp. 220 and 330, n. 40, however, Fichtenau seems not to agree with Chaume; he there states that Bigo was "perhaps a son-in-law of Louis" the Pious and hence that Alpaïs was Louis's daughter. See also Simson, *op. cit.*, I, 11, nn. 7, 8.

51. The marriage took place ca. 794 when Louis was sixteen years old. Irmingard, the mother of Lothair, Pepin, and Louis (the German), died in 818 (see ch. 31 below). Fichtenau, *op. cit.*, 244, cites some evidence that the memory of Irmingard was execrated and that she was blamed for the cruelty inflicted upon young Bernard of Italy (see ch. 30:1 below), acting thus to insure lands for her sons, in particular for Lothair; that her death was looked upon as a divine judgment; and that she was pictured (along with others, among them Bigo) as in hell suffering the torments of the damned. There are at least two possibilities here: (1) there is confusion of Irmingard with the later Empress Judith, or (2) there is deliberate propaganda in behalf of Judith and her faction against the sons of Irmingard.

52. "claris ortam natalibus." Cf. Aldhelm, *De laude virginum*, 1779: "claris natalibus ortam." See Manitius, "Zu dem Epos," 618.

53. See ch. 14:1 below for his part in the siege of Tortosa in 809.

54. 11 Nov. 799.

55. "ibidemque infulas imperatorias suscipiente." Cf. Ammianus Marcellinus, *op. cit.*, XV, 6, 3: "antequam infulas susciperet principatus." See Manitius, "Zu deutschen Geschichtsquellen," 71.

56. See ch. 13:2 below. He was later replaced by Hamur as Saracen governor of Barcelona. In 801 he advanced against Narbonne, but he was captured and carried first before Louis, then before Charles. His former city was then betrayed by his own followers.

57. Exact identification unknown.

58. "ut ferunt." See Einhard, *op. cit.*, 7, 8.

59. See Prologue, note 14, above.

60. See also ch. 16 below for Liutard's part in the campaign against Tortosa in 811.

61. "poenas . . . pro talibus ausis dederunt." Cf. Vergil, *Aeneid*, II, 535–37: "At tibi . . . pro talibus . . . praemia reddant." See Manitius, "Zu dem Epos," 618.

62. "divisoque in tres partes exercitu." Cf. *Annales regni Francorum, anno* 824: "et inde diviso in tres partes exercitu." See Manitius, "Zu deutschen Geschichtsquellen," 73.

63. See Prologue, note 14, above.

64. "detracto ostiis coria." Cf. Mela, *De situ orbis libri III*, III, 9: "detracta occisis coria." See Manitius, "Zu deutschen Geschichtsquellen," 73.

65. "qui vero spe animabantur inani." Cf. Nithard, *De dissensionibus filiorum Ludovici pii*, I, 5: "eadem . . . spe animatus." See Manitius, "Zu deutschen Geschichtsquellen," 73.

66. See note 56 above.

67. On Bera, see ch. 14:1 below (on the campaign against Tortosa, 809); ch. 15:1 (appointed with others to construct

boats for use in the Tortosa campaign, 810); ch. 33 (failure
in duel with Sanila and exile in Rouen, 820); and ch. 41:1 (his
son Willemundus in revolt with Aizo against Louis, 827).

68. "ad propria remeavit." Cf. Ammianus Marcellinus, *op.
cit.*, XVII, 10, 9: "ad propria remeare est permissus." See Manitius, "Zu deutschen Geschichtsquellen," 71.

69. See note 5 above; also ch. 20:1 below (his death).

70. Should, of course, be "the *emperor* his father."

71. 2 Feb. 809.

72. Ash Wednesday, 809, was 4 March; Easter was 19 April.

73. "cum quanto visum est bellico apparatu." Cf. Einhard,
op. cit., 9: "quam maximo poterat belli apparatu." See Manitius,
"Zu deutschen Geschichtsquellen," 72.

74. On Isembard, see ch. 16 below (at Tortosa, 811);
Adhemar, Prologue, note 14, above; Bera, note 67 above;
Burrellus, note 53 above.

75. "Bramble Villa"—unidentified.

76. Unidentified; possibly located near the Ysabena river?
Another text reads *Valla-Ibana.*

77. "praeruptis . . . cingatur montibus." Cf. Vergil, *Aeneid,*
I, 105: "praeruptus aquae mons."

78. "praeceperat namque . . . fabricari naves." Cf. Justin,
Historiarum ex Trogo Pompeio excerptarum libri, II, 12: "cc
[ducentas] naves fabricaverant." See Manitius, "Zu deutschen
Geschichtsquellen," 70.

79. "in omnibus fluminibus quae mari influebant." Cf.
Nithard, *op. cit.*, II, 6: "quo Sequana mare influit." See Manitius,
"Zu deutschen Geschichtsquellen," 73.

80. Unidentified.

81. Last mention of Ademar; see note 59 above.

82. To a North American, this has the ring of Indian warfare.

83. Heribert, ch. 17:1 below (emissary of Charles, sent by

Louis against Huesca, 812); ch. 45:1 (brother of Bernard of Barcelona, blinded by Louis's rebelling sons, 830).

84. "ut cives illius a spe deciderant." Cf. Livy, *Historiarum libri*, XXXII, 26: "postquam a spe societatis Prusiae decidit." See Manitius, "Zu deutschen Geschichtsquellen," 70.

85. "infractosque suos adverso Marte cernentes." Cf. Vergil, *Aeneid*, XII, 1f.: "Turnus ut infractos adverso Martes Latinos / Defecisse videt." See Manitius, "Zu dem Epos," 618.

86. See note 83 above.

87. "propius muros accedentes." Cf. Nepos, *Miltiades*, VII, 2: "propius murus accessit." See Manitius, "Zu deutschen Geschichtsquellen," 70.

88. "primum lacessere dein missilibus incessere temptant." Cf. Ammianus Mercellinus, *op. cit.*, XIV, 2, 5: "missilibus obvios eminens lacessens." See Manitius, "Zu deutschen Geschichtsquellen," 71.

89. "ad quorum pervicatiam opprimendum ire publica utilitas postularet." Cf. Ammianus Marcellinus, *op. cit.*, XVII, 13, 1: "ad . . . Sarmatas . . . ocius signa transferri utilitas publica flagitabat." See Manitius, "Zu deutschen Geschichtsquellen," 71.

90. "omnes laudibus prosecuntur." Cf. Livy, *op. cit.*, IX, 8: "Cum omnes laudibus modo prosequentes virum." See Manitius, "Zu deutschen Geschichtsquellen," 70.

91. "ab ineunti aetate." Cf. Cicero, *Orationes*, I, 21: "ab ineunti aetate." See Manitius, "Zu deutschen Geschichtsquellen," 71.

92. See Cassiodorus, *An Introduction to Divine and Human Readings*, trans. and ed. L. W. Jones (New York: Columbia University Press, 1946).

93. At this point in some MSS there is a very interesting interpolation: "the monastery of Saints Mary and Peter at Ferrières which was anciently called Bethlehem, in the court of which his father Pepin killed a lion; and he himself was

honorably consecrated as king in the same church by Stephen
[? III, pope 768–772], the Roman pope. . . ." Important in its
own right, this passage was obviously not in the original. First,
Ferrières is not in Aquitaine; and, secondly, the phrase, "his
father Pepin," indicates that Charles the Great, not Louis the
Pious, is the subject of the allusion.

94. Sancta Maria de Regula at Limoges.

95. At Poitiers.

96. That is, on the Orbieu river. Of the twenty-five founda-
tions here named, all are known except Devera, Deutera, Vadala,
and St. Pascentius; Tykocinski, *Quellenkritische Beiträge*, 22–34.
St. Filibert is, of course, Hermoutier or Noirmoutier; St. Florent,
St. Florent-le-Vieil; St. Theotfrid, St. Chafre; and St. Lawrence,
St. Laurent-de-la-Carberesse.

97. This reminds one of St. Louis IX. See John of Joinville,
Life of St. Louis, trans. René Hague (New York: Sheed and
Ward, 1955), 37f.

98. Also spelled Erkanbaldus.   99. Cf. Matt. 25:15–23.

100. Pepin died on 24 June 810.

101. Charles died on 6 Dec. 811.

102. "spes universitatis potiundae in eum assurgebat." This
language suggests an element of greed or ambition as a fault
of Louis; cf. note 50 above.

103. Emending *Gerrico capis praelato* to *Gerrico in capsis
praelato* has been suggested, but the text as it stands seems more
reasonable. See Simson, *op. cit.,* I, 2, n. 8.

104. "quod pater cum iam in senilem vergeret aetatem."
Cf. Ammianus Marcellinus, *op. cit.,* XIV, 6, 4: "iamque vergens
in senium." See Manitius, "Zu deutschen Geschichtsquellen," 71.

105. Reminiscent of, but not verbally identical with, Eph. 3:20.

106. "et tandem imperiali cum diademate coronavit." On 13
Sept. 813.

107. "et lector decubuit . . . diem ultimum clausit." Cf.
Annales Fuldenses, anno 840 (of Louis): "12 Kal. Iul. diem

ultimum clausit." Also *ibid.*, *anno* 882. See Manitius, "Zu deutschen Geschichtsquellen," 73.

108. Cf. the poetic lament on Charles's death translated by Howard Mumford Jones in P. S. Allen, *The Romanesque Lyric* (Chapel Hill: University of North Carolina Press, 1928), 224f.

109. Ecclus. 30:4.   110. 28 Jan. 814.

111. The second precise date given in the text; cf. note 17 above.

112. 2 Feb. 814.

PART II

1. Cf. Ermoldus Nigellus, *De rebus gestis Ludovici*, II, 741–743.

2. Louis's sisters?

3. "vir undecumque doctissimus." Cf. Einhard, *Vita Karoli*, 25: "virum undecumque doctissimum" (of Alcuin, not Theodulf). On Theodulf, see also chs. 26:2 and 29:2 below. Of Spanish origin, he was born about 750 and died in 821. Although an intimate of the court, he was implicated in the revolt of Bernard of Italy in 817 and was banished the following year. He was restored in the year in which he died. The familiar Palm Sunday hymn, "Gloria, laus et honor," is attributed to him. A convenient summary of the known facts of his life and select bibliography are given in G. E. McCracken and Allen Cabaniss, eds., *Early Medieval Theology* (Philadelphia: Westminster Press, 1957), 379–81; consult also Ann Freeman, "Theodulf of Orleans and the *Libri Carolini*," *Speculum*, XXXII, No. 4 (Oct. 1957), 663–705; Hans Liebeschütz, "Theodulf of Orleans and the Problem of the Carolingian Renaissance," in D. J. Gordon, ed., *Fritz Saxl, 1890–1948: A Volume of Memorial Essays from His Friends in England* (Edinburgh: Thomas Nelson and Sons, 1957), 77–92; R. H. Schwoebel, "The Carolingian Theocracy and Bishop Theodulf" (an unpublished M.A. thesis, University of Mississippi, 1954). See Manitius, "Zu deutschen Geschichtsquellen," 72.

4. I.e., notice of Charles's death.

5. On Wala, see also chs. 35:3, 45:1, 55:1, 56:2 below; on his older brother, Adalard, chs. 34:2, 36; and on their brother Barnarius, ch. 34:2. These men were sons of Bernard, a natural

son of Charles Martel and hence first cousins of Charles the
Great. Reared at the court of Pepin and Charlemagne, Adalard
became a monk at Corbie in 773. In 775 he went to Monte
Cassino, but he was soon recalled to Frankland to become abbot
of Corbie. Beginning in 796 he served for a period as adviser
to King Pepin of Italy and from 810 to 814 as guardian of
Pepin's son and successor, young King Bernard. Thence Adalard
returned again to Corbie, but Emperor Louis, upon his accession,
banished him and his brothers. They were recalled from exile
in 821. Adalard founded New Corvey at Paderborn and served
once more as abbot of Corbie until his death in 826.

Not only were Adalard and Wala first cousins of the great
Charles but also of the famous St. William of Gellone, count
of Toulouse (see Part I, n. 35, above). Wala was indeed married
to William's daughter, probably Rothlindis, and hence a brother-
in-law of Bernard of Barcelona (see note 126 below). By the
time of his banishment he was a widower and was tonsured.
Later he succeeded his brother Adalard as abbot of Corbie and
also served for a while as abbot of Bobbio. He was responsible
for the mission of Ansgar to Schleswig. His strong influence
at the court of Louis is evident in the text as cited at the
beginning of this note. [According to Fichtenau, *Das karolingische Imperium*, 334, n. 77, citing M. Chaume, *Les origines
du duché de Bourgogne*, I, 151, n. 2, Wala and his brothers
were also first cousins of Empress Judith.]

For what they are worth, there are lives of Adalard and
Wala by Paschasius Radbertus, MPL cxxi, 1507C–56C, 1559D–
1650B. See the old but useful A. Himly, *Wala et Louis le
débonnaire* (Paris: Didot, 1849); C. Rodenberg, *Die vita Walae
als historischer Quelle* (Göttingen, 1887); Arrigo Solmi, *Stato
e Chiesa secondo gli scritti politici da Carlomagno fino al con-
cilio di Worms* (Modena, 1901).

6. "summi apud Karolum imperatorem habitus loci." Cf.
Nithard, *De dissensionibus filiorum Ludovici pii*, IV, 5: "et

apud magnum Karolum merito magni habebatur." See Manitius, "Zu deutschen Geschichtsquellen," 73.

7. "et die tricesimo postquam ab Aquitania promovit." Cf. *Annales regni Francorum, anno* 814: "tricesimo die postquam id [i.e., Charles's death] acciderat . . . venit."

8. Accepting the statement in *Annales regni Francorum* (see preceding note), the date would be 27 Feb. 814.

9. The laxity of the lives of Louis's sisters may be illustrated by reference to Bertha whose lover was Angilbert and of whom the historian Nithard was born. See, *inter alia*, Duckett, *Alcuin*, 93–95; Simson, *op. cit.*, I, 13f.

10. Odilo, a duke of Bavaria; Hiltrud, a daughter of Charles Martel (hence great-aunt of Louis the Pious). Odilo and Hiltrud were the parents of that Tassilo of Bavaria who created so many difficulties for his cousin, Emperor Charles.

11. On Wala, see note 5 above. Warnarius is mentioned only here in this *Vita*. (Bernard of Barcelona, note 136 below, had a brother named Guarnarius.) On Lantbert (count of Nantes), see also chs. 39:2, 44:2, 52:2 below. He is probably to be identified with the Lambert of chs. 45:1, 56:2 below. On Ingobert, see ch. 15:1 above.

12. A curious name for the place and period; mentioned only here in this *Vita*. The Latin, *ad misericordiam*, is probably corrupt; I have therefore translated as though it were *a misericordia*. For another emendation, see Simson, *op. cit.*, I, 15, n. 1.

13. "metropolitanorum . . . subdivisit superscriptione nominum quarum partes fuere viginti et una. Quod autem ornatui condecebat regio." Cf. Einhard, *Vita Karoli*, 33: "et ornatui regio . . . partes subdividendo de duabus partibus XX et unam partem fecit." Cf. Thegan, *Vita Ludovici imperatoris*, 8; F. N. Estey, "Charlemagne's Silver Celestial Table," *Speculum*, XVIII, No. 1 (Jan. 1943), 112–17. See Manitius, "Zu deutschen Geschichtsquellen," 72.

14. "quae cuncta domnus imperator Hluduicus ut scripta

relegit operis executione complevit." Cf. Einhard, *op. cit.*, 33: "haec omnia filius eius Hluduicus . . . inspecto eodem breviario . . . adimplere curavit." See Manitius, "Zu deutschen Geschichtsquellen," 72.

15. "legationes ad patrem destinatas ad se autem venientes et susceptas diligenter audivit, dapsiliter curavit, sumptuose muneratas remisit. Inter quas vel praecipua fuit imperatoris Constantinopolitani." Cf. *Annales regni Francorum, anno* 814: "legationes gentium quae ad patrem venerant auditas absolvit, alias ad patrem quidem missas ad se vero venientes suscepit. Inter quas praecipua fuit legatio de Constantinopoli directa." The Eastern emperor was Michael I Rhangabé (811–13). See Nickel, *Untersuchungen*, 7.

16. On this mission, see Allen Cabaniss, *Amalarius of Metz* (Amsterdam: North-Holland Publishing Co., 1954), 33–42 and the literature therein cited.

17. "misit missos suos." Cf. *Annales regni Francorum, anno* 814: "Hluduicus legatos suos . . . direxit." See Nickel, *Untersuchungen*, 7.

18. Leo V the Armenian (813–20); see also chs. 27, 34:1 below.

19. Bishop of Reggio (in Lombardy), 814–15 June 835; see also ch. 25:3 below.

20. See also ch. 25:3 below.

21. "petens amicitiarum societatem et renovationem antiquarum simul et pacti confirmationem." Cf. *Annales regni Francorum, anno* 814: "ob renovandam secum amicitiam et praedictum pactum confirmandum direxit." See Nickel, *Untersuchungen*, 7.

22. "Generalem conventum Aquisgrani habuit et per universas regni sui partes fideles misit." Cf. *Annales regni Francorum, anno* 814: "habitoque Aquisgrani generali populi sui conventu . . . legatos in omnes regni sui partes dimisit." See Nickel, *Untersuchungen*, 7.

23. Son of Louis's brother Pepin and possibly illegitimate, on whom see also chs. 25:1, 26:2, 29:2, 30:1, 35:1 below; a very important person in any consideration of Louis's psychology. Simson, *op. cit.*, I, 335, n. 4, states that Bertha, sister of Bernard of Barcelona, was the wife of Charlemagne's son Pepin and hence mother of Bernard of Italy. On the other hand, J. Calmette, *De Bernardo sancti Guillelmi filio* (*?–844*) (Toulouse: Privat, 1902), 14f., lists only three sisters of Bernard of Barcelona, none of whom was named Bertha.

24. "Bernhardum nepotem suum iamdudum regem Italiae ad se evocatum et oboedienter parentem amplis muneribus donatum ad proprium remisit regnum." Cf. *Annales regni Francorum, anno* 814: "Bernhardum regem Italiae nepotem suum ad se evocatum muneribus donatum in regnum remisit." (Observe that the word *nepos* is here used to signify nephew.) To this point ch. 23 is based on the *Annales regni Francorum, anno* 814, but the remainder of the chapter differs since the *Annales* imply that Grimoald was present in person. See Nickel, *Untersuchungen*, 7.

25. This is the first mention of these three sons who played such an important part in the events of Louis's life and reign.

26. Heriold (Harold) reappears in chs. 25:2, 27, 40:1, 42:3 below.

27. "ad quem summa totius regni Danorum pertinere videbatur." Cf. *Annales regni Francorum, anno* 803: "et summam totius regni . . . habere praecepit." See Manitius, "Zu deutschen Geschichtsquellen," 73.

28. The sons of Godefrid, challenging Heriold's rule, reappear in chs. 27, 29:1, 42:3 below.

29. "talibus habenis . . . coerceri, ne . . . in . . . procacitatem ferrentur." Cf. Nepos, *Timoleon*, V. 2: "qui procacitatem hominis manibus coercere conarentur." See Manitius, "Zu deutschen Geschichtsquellen," 70.

30. Elected pope on 26 Dec. 795 and buried on 12 June 816,

according to Pius Bonifacius Gams, *Series episcoporum ecclesiae catholicae* (reprint; Graz: Akademische Druck- u. Verlagsanstalt, 1957), ii, but ch. 26:2 of this *Vita* gives his death as occurring on 25 May 816.

31. "supplicio addixerit capitali." Cf. Ammianum Marcellinus, *Rerum gestarum libri*, XV, 3, 2: "capitalibus addixere suppliciis." See Manitius, "Zu deutschen Geschichtsquellen," 71.

32. Cf. ch. 40:1 below, which mentions a Gerald, guardian of the Pannonian frontiers.

33. Cf. 37:1 below. Gams, *op. cit.*, ix, lists John as bishop only from 823 to 826.

34. See also ch. 27 below; possibly to be identified with Theodore the *primicerius* of chs. 34:2, 37:1 below.

35. Later a duke of Friuli and guardian of the Pannonian frontiers; cf. chs. 32:2, 40:2, 42:1 below.

36. In Schleswig.

37. "nolentibus . . . et pugnae se credere." Cf. Vergil, *Aeneid*, V, 382: "si nemo audet se credere pugnae." See Manitius, "Zu dem Epos," 618.

38. Hakam I, emir of Córdoba, 796–822; cf. also chs. 26:3, 34:1 below; full name El Hakam Abul Aas.

39. *domocultas;* see DuCange, *Glossarium*, s.v. *Domus* 2: "Praedium domo ad commanendum colonis apta instructum: nos *Ferme*, vocamus."

40. 25 May, but see note 30 above.

41. Stephen V was elected pope on 22 June 816. He crowned Louis the Pious on 5 Oct., and died on 24 or 25 Jan. 817; see ch. 27 below.

42. John II, bishop 811–19.

43. On these *laudes*, see Ernst Kantorowicz, *Laudes Regiae: A Study in Liturgical Acclamations and Mediaeval Ruler Worship* (Berkeley and Los Angeles: University of California Press, 1946).

44. On 5 Oct. 816. Thegan, *op. cit.*, 17, says that the pope

brought the crown from Rome; and Ermoldus Nigellus, *op. cit.*, II, 1077, says that it was "the crown of Constantine." Rheims was the place where Clovis, first king of the Franks, was baptized in 496 by St. Remigius. See *Butler's Lives of the Saints*, ed. H. Thurston and D. Attwater (New York: Kenedy and Sons, 1956), IV, 1-3. On the coronation, see Simson, *op. cit.*, I, 73f.

45. For whatever it is worth, Thegan, *op. cit.*, 19, in language similar to that used by Einhard, *op. cit.*, 22-25, of Charlemagne, describes Louis as of medium height, with large, bright eyes, shining countenance, long, straight nose, lips neither too thick nor too thin, strong chest, broad shoulders, muscular arms, long hands and straight fingers, long, graceful legs, long feet, and manly voice; as strong, agile, and active, temperate in food and drink, modest in dress, addicted to hunting, and excessively generous, but always unsmiling.

46. Apparently the same as Cadalus, ch. 31, and Duke Cadolach [Cadolh] of Friuli, ch. 32:2, below.

47. According to *Annales regni Francorum, anno* 817, he was a *nepos*, grandson (or nephew; see note 24 above), of Unruoch; see the following note.

48. This sentence is clarified by *Annales regni Francorum, anno* 817: "quem [Niciforum], quia Cadolah . . . non aderat, et tamen brevi venturus putabatur, adventum illius iussit operiri; quo veniente ratio inter eum et legatum imperatoris de questionibus, quas idem detulit, habita est, neque sine illorum praesentia finiri posse videbatur, illo decernenda differtur, missusque adhoc cum Cadolane et praedicto legato in Dalmatiam Albigarius, Unrochi nepos." See Nickel, *Untersuchungen*, 8f.

49. 7 Feb.; but according to Theodor von Oppolzer, *Canon de Finsternisse* (Vienna: Karl Gerold's Sohn, 1887), 356, the eclipse occurred on 5 Feb.

50. 24 or 25 Jan. 817. On the phrase, see Part I, note 107, above.

51. Paschal I, consecrated pope on 25 Jan. 817 and died ca. 14 May 824; see also chs. 34:1, 36, 37:1 below.

52. That is, predecessors of both the pope and the emperor.

53. Holy (or Maundy) Thursday, 9 April 817.

54. 29 April 817.

55. The books, *De institutione canonicorum* and *De institutione sanctimonialium*, attributed to Amalarius in MPL, CV, 821–934, 935–72. See Simson, *op. cit.*, I, 90–94.

56. Reading *sicut recultus ipse fatetur* instead of the alternative *sicut reclusus ipse fatetur*, which is virtually meaningless.

57. "debita cum laude." Cf. Einhard, *op. cit., praef.*: "sine litteris ac debita laude." See Manitius, "Zu deutschen Geschichtsquellen," 72.

58. I.e., the well-known Benedict of Aniane. See *Butler's Lives of the Saints*, I, 309f.

59. There are many editions of this *Regula.* An interesting Latin and Anglo-Saxon interlinear version was edited for the Early English Text Society by H. Logeman, *The Rule of S. Benet* (London: Trübner, 1888).

60. "ut quicumque ex servili ordine . . . primum manumittantur a propriis dominis." Cf. Justin, *Historiarum ex Trogo Pompeio excerptarum libri*, III, 5: "ut ad supplementum exercitus servos suos manumitterent." See Manitius, "Zu deutschen Geschichtsquellen," 70.

61. *mansus;* see DuCange, *Glossarium*, s.v. *Mansus*, one definition of which is: "quantitas terrae, quae sufficit duobus bobus in anno ad laborandum."

62. Note the doctrine of the *corpus diaboli.*

63. Bishop of Verona, ca. 799–840; see also ch. 52:1 below.

64. *Annales regni Francorum, anno* 822, mention him as count of Brescia; and *anno* 824, as duke of Spoleto.

65. "regalium primus amicorum." Apparently a title of office, as e.g., in II Macc. 10:13.

66. His death is recorded in the next chapter.

67. Is he to be identified with a man of the same name in ch. 61:2 below?

68. Bishop, 816–18; name also given elsewhere as Walfred.

69. See note 3 above.

70. Easter, 28 Mar. 818; cf. Thegan, *op. cit.*, 22.

71. Nithard, *op. cit.*, I, *praef.*, states that Count Bertmund of Lyons supervised the execution of this sentence, which took place on 15 April 818.

72. Note how the author tries to exonerate the emperor of young Bernard's death. On Irmingard's blame in this cruelty, see Simson, *op. cit.*, I, 124f.

73. This would be 7 Oct. 818, but other sources make the date 3 Oct.

74. This would be 24 June, but Oppolzer, *op. cit.*, 194, gives the date as 7 July 818, the eclipse being a "ringforming-total, central eclipse."

75. Croats (?).   76. Dwellers near the Timok river.

77. A troublesome chieftain who reappears in chs. 32:2, 32:3, 34:1, 35:2 below.

78. Here described as a king, but in ch. 40:1 below as a duke of the Obotrites. His father, Trasco, is mentioned in *Annales regni Francorum, anno* 908, as having been slain by the men of Godefrid, king of the Danes.

79. "Lupus Centulli cognomento." I.e., Lupus Centulli or as in the text above.

80. Werinus (Warinus, Guerinus) is also mentioned in chs. 44:1, 49:2, 51, 52:3 below. A Warinus was one of the magnates of Carloman who submitted to Charlemagne in 771 (*Annales regni Francorum, anno* 771). Is this Berengar the same as the son of Count Unruoch mentioned in ch. 57 below?

81. The marriage took place at Aachen in Feb. 819. Judith, a significant influence on Louis's life and reign, is mentioned further in chs. 37:2, 44, 52:1, 54:3, 59, 61:3, 62:1, 63:2, below. Little is known of Judith's life before her appearance at court

and marriage to the emperor. She was born ca. 800 or later of
a very wealthy family of Alamannia (not of Bavaria, as usually
stated). Her father was Count Welf and her mother was Eigilwi
(or Heilwich), a noble Saxon. Her outstanding beauty, grace,
and charm, as well as her learning, were the admiration of her
contemporaries. She immediately became a strong influence at
court and over the emperor who was perhaps more than twice
her age at the marriage.

Her first child was a daughter, Hildegard or Adelheid, and
so was her third, Gisela. But the birth of her middle child, a son,
Charles (known to history as "the Bald"), on 13 June 823, was
the signal for a period of bitter struggle to secure for him a
place equal to that already assigned to his three elder half-
brothers. In one way or another Judith was able to fill the
palace with her partisans. Her brothers, Conrad and Rudolf,
became important functionaries; her widowed mother was made
abbess of Chelles, the great foundation where Charlemagne's
sister Gisela had spent her latter years; her sister Emma was
married to the emperor's son, Louis of Bavaria; and Abbot
Wala, her mother's first cousin (?), was recalled to power.
Wala's brother-in-law, Bernard of Barcelona (see note 136 below), imperial chamberlain for a while, may have become
Judith's lover, or so the anti-Judith faction loudly proclaimed.
(Fichtenau, *op. cit.*, 334, n. 78, citing Chaume, *op. cit.*, I, 152,
n. 3, surely errs in believing that Dhuoda, wife of Bernard of
Barcelona, was Judith's sister.) In the eyes of Walafrid Strabo,
Judith was the "Rachel" of the court; but in the eyes of
Paschasius Radbertus she was a reincarnation of Queen Brunhild,
persecutor of St. Columban; see his *Vita Walae seu epitaphium
Arsenii*, II, 21 (MPL CXX, 1643D–44A).

The chief events of her career during the lifetime of Louis
the Pious are, in the main, recorded in our anonymous *Vita
Hludovici*. She died at Tours in 843 after having been deprived
by her son of all her fortune (? *substantia*). According to re-

ports, the long overdue full-scale biography of Judith is being prepared as a Ph.D. thesis at the University of Chicago by Mrs. Bernard Fischer. See Simson, *op. cit.*, I, 145–48.

82. See Part I, note 107, above.

83. "Qui cum primum in provinciam venisset et Carantanas ingrederetur partes. . . ."

84. Mentioned also in chs. 33, 34:1 below. According to *Annales regni Francorum*, his death occurred in 821.

85. "trina partitione divisae." Cf. Einhard, *op. cit.*, 33: "trina divisione partitus est." See Manitius, "Zu deutschen Geschichtsquellen," 72.

86. Sanila (Senila, Sanilo, Senilo). Is this the same as the Count Sanila whose beheading is related in ch. 52:3 below?

87. "equestri praelio." I.e., on horseback.

88. 1 May 821.

89. Peter I, 826–?; see also ch. 56:1 below. Gams, *op. cit.*, xi.

90. His violent death is mentioned in ch. 37 below; undoubtedly not to be confused with a "master of troops" named Leo and also referred to in that chapter.

91. Many spellings of this name.

92. Michael II the Amorian, 820–829; mentioned in chs. 41:2, 42:2 below.

93. Count of Tours, closely associated with Count Matfrid of Orléans (see note 137 below) as great magnates of Frankland and ultimately as leaders of the aristocratic anti-court party; died in 826. See chs. 41:1, 56:2 below.

94. According to *Annales regni Francorum, anno* 821, Florus was a papal sacristan (*superista*).

95. Note the superlatives: "in hoc conventu quam maxime quanta in eius esset pectore manifestissime patuit."

96. On Adalard, see note 5 above.

97. See note 5 above.

98. Theodosius I (346–395) had massacred seven thousand Macedonians in 390 in revenge for a tumult. St. Ambrose, bishop

of Milan, refused him entrance to the church until he had done penance for eight months. Fichtenau, *op. cit.*, 218, observes quite rightly that Theodosius's penance was by no means voluntary and was therefore different from Louis's penance.

99. See also ch. 39:1 below.

100. *Annales regni Francorum, anno* 822, call him indeed "master of the *ostiarii.*"

101. The daughter of Theotbert was named Ingeltrud and was distantly related to Pepin. Their common ancestor was Pepin of Heristal (d. 714): she was a great-great-granddaughter and he was a great-great-great-grandson.

102. "magna inter se alterna vi vertebant." Cf. Vergil, *Georgics*, IV, 174: "Illi inter sese magna vi brachia tollunt." See Manitius, "Zu dem Epos," 618.

103. According to *Annales regni Francorum, anno* 823, Mileguastus was the elder.

104. See preceding chapter.

105. 5 April 823.

106. Presumably Adalard, abbot of Corbie; see note 5 above.

107. The thirty-ninth bishop of Metz, translated from the see of Le Mans in Jan. 819.

108. See Part I, note 65, above.

109. The fortieth bishop of Metz and a natural son of Charlemagne. Designated to the see in June 823, as here recorded, he was ordained priest on 12 June, when scarcely twenty-three years of age (according to Fichtenau, *op. cit.*, 232). Consecrated on Sunday, 30 June 823, he reigned thirty-four years, five months, and seven days, dying on 8 Dec. 855. He was interred in the church of St. John, Metz, on 13 Dec. 855. Much of the time he was also archchaplain of the sacred palace. Completely loyal to his brother, Louis the Pious, he was very influential at court. See also chs. 49:2, 54:1, 63, 64 below.

110. "ut omnes id velle nullus nolle reperiretur." A play on words which can fortunately be conveyed in translation.

111. *Annales regni Francorum, anno* 823: "Hunfridus comes Curiensis."

112. "accusationi opponentes excusationem." Another play on words which can be translated as such.

113. 1 November 823.

114. *Annales regni Francorum, anno* 823: "In this year a number of portents occurred (so it is said): an earthquake at the palace of Aix, the fast of a twelve-year-old girl from all food for ten months at Commercy, twenty-five villas in Saxony burned by fire from heaven, lightning-bolts falling for a long time from a clear sky, harvests destroyed in many places by shattering hail, stones of great weight falling with the hail, houses struck from the sky, men and animals killed by crushing blows of lightning. . . ." *Ibid., anno* 825, relate that the girl, who began her fast at Easter, 5 April, 823, finally broke it about 1 Nov. 825.

115. Known to history as *Carolus Calvus,* Charles the Bald, born on 13 June 823.

116. *Annales Bertiniani, anno* 836, recount that Asenarius, "count of hither Gascony," died a "horrible death."

117. "solitam loci perfidiam habitatorumque genuinam experti sunt fraudem." Cf. Einhard, *op. cit.,* 9: "Wasconicam perfidiam parumper in redeundo contigit experiri." See Manitius, "Zu deutschen Geschichtsquellen," 72.

118. *Annales regni Francorum, anno* 824, make the relationship uncertain: "*quasi* qui consanguineus eorum esset. . . ." Italics mine. See Simson, *op. cit.,* I, 224f.

119. See chs. 35:3, 36 above.

120. Eugenius II (May or July 824—d. August 827); see also chs. 40:2, 41:2 below.

121. "iustitiam . . . aequa lance penderent." Cf. Pliny, *Historiae naturalis libri,* VII, 5: "Is . . . vitam aequa lance pensitabit." See Manitius, "Zu deutschen Geschichtsquellen," 71.

122. *Annales regni Francorum, anno* 825: "circa medium Maium."

123. "oboedientiamque multis prosequentes verbis." Cf. Cicero, *Tusculan Orations*, II, 25: "honorificisque verbis prosecutus." See Manitius, "Zu deutschen Geschichtsquellen," 71.

124. Emending "ab hoc conventu" (referring to the August assembly just mentioned) to read "ab illo conventu" (referring to the May assembly with which this chapter began). See Nickel, *Untersuchungen*, 12f.

125. 1 Feb. 826.   126. 1 June 826.

127. Elaborately and interestingly described in Ermoldus Nigellus, *op. cit.*, IV, *ad init.*, but located therein at Ingelheim near Mainz.

128. "sacrorum scriniorum praelato."

129. This organ was a notable event in Frankland mentioned by the annals, Walafrid Strabo, Einhard, Ermoldus Nigellus, and others. Judith could apparently play the instrument. For all that, however, there had been organs in Frankland since 757 when one was received by King Pepin (Charlemagne's father) from Emperor Constantine V of Byzantium. See Simson, *op. cit.*, I, 266f.

130. Königshofen on the Sala?

131. See also ch. 41:1 below.

132. See also ch. 45:1 below. Archchaplain (819–22), abbot of St. Denis, St. Germain, and St. Médard, he was in 830 a partisan of Louis's sons and was consequently banished to New Korvey in Saxony. Soon recalled, however, he was reinstated at St. Denis and St. Médard. He was commissioned by Louis in 835 to write the life of St. Denis. This work, popularizing the identity of St. Denis with the Biblical Dionysius the Areopagite (Acts 17:34), was attacked by John Scotus Eriugena. Hilduin died on 22 Nov. 840. Fichtenau, *op. cit.*, 334, n. 78 (following Chaume, *op. cit.*, I, 551), claims that Hilduin was

a brother of Count Odo of Orléans, who was later father-in-law
of Charles the Bald. Cf. also, Buchner, "Enstehungszeit."

133. Mark 9:23.

134. "ad quos motus comprimendos nostrosque roborandos."
Annales regni Francorum, anno 817: "ad quos motus comprimendos." See Manitius, "Zu deutschen Geschichtsquellen," 73.

135. See also ch. 45:1 below (and on Donatus, ch. 59:1, below).
Helisachar had been Louis's chancellor in Aquitaine and remained for a while as imperial chancellor. Abbot of St. Riquier,
he wrote two books of chronicles from the beginning of the
world to the Empress Judith; see Edmund Bishop, *Liturgica
Historica* (Oxford: Clarendon, 1918), 333–48.

136. Very important; see chs. 43–47, 49:2, 51:1, 57, 59:1, below. The detailed work on this person is Calmette, *De Bernardo
sancti Guillelmi filio;* more briefly, Allen Cabaniss, "The Woes
of Dhuoda or France's First Woman of Letters," *Mississippi
Quarterly*, XI, No. 1 (Winter 1958), 38–49. Bernard was executed in 844 by command of Charles the Bald.

137. On Hugo, see note 93 above. On Matfrid, see also chs.
44:1, 52:2, 56:2 below.

138. "tandiu morae innexae sunt moris" (delays were added
to delays as long as possible); or interpreting *moris* as *Mauris*
and translating "delays were granted to the Moors." In any case,
the ultimate meaning of both is the same.

139. Presumably the Northern Lights (*Aurora borealis.*)

140. The only pope of this name.

141. Gregory IV, 827–44; see chs. 55:2, 56:1 and 56:2, below.

142. Einhard (ca. 770—14 March 840), born in Maingau,
reared at Fulda, tutored by Alcuin at the court of Charlemagne
and Louis. Short of stature, but skilled in architecture, he became
a favorite of the emperors, by whom he was called "Beseleel."
He retired from court in 830 to become lay abbot of Seligen-
stadt (his wife, Imma, died in 836). His letters, *Vita Karoli,*

and *Translatio sanctorum Marcellini et Petri* are precious sources not only of historical details, but also of the life of the times; Manitius, *Geschichte*, I, 639–46; Laistner, *op. cit.*, 273–75, and elsewhere. On the value of Einhard's work, especially the *Vita Karoli*, see, *inter alia*, George Nordmeyer, "On the OHG Isidor and Its Significance for Early German Prose," *PMLA*, LXXIII, No. 1 (March 1958), 23–35, especially pp. 34f., and the literature there cited.

143. Although ch. 41 is based on *Annales regni Francorum*, *anno* 827, the annals do not mention the name of Einhard; see Einhard, *The History of the Translation of the Blessed Martyrs of Christ Marcellinus and Peter*, English version by Barrett Wendell (Cambridge: Harvard University Press, 1926), *passim*.

144. Matfrid and Hugo among others?

145. As, e.g., in chs. 45:2, 46:1.

146. Bishop, 817—d. 25 June 831; see L. Duchesne, *Fastes épiscopaux de l'ancienne Gaule*, III (Paris: Fontemoing et Cie., 1915), 112f.

147. "a transmarinis partibus redeuntes humanissime se susceptos a Michael retulerunt." Cf. *Annales regni Francorum*, *anno* 828: "missi et sicut ipsi inde reversi rettulerunt honorifice suscepti sunt." See Nickel, *Untersuchungen*, 7.

148. The Latin text is in indirect discourse, but I have taken the liberty of rendering it as direct.

149. "igni iniecto." Cf. Ammianus Marcellinus, *op. cit.*, XVIII, 7, 4: "iniecto igni." Once again I have taken a liberty in translating. See Manitius, "Zu deutschen Geschichtsquellen," 71.

150. The same noble may perhaps be mentioned in chs. 52:1, 59:1, below.

151. This incident also appears in *Annales regni Francorum*, *anno* 828. The name of Boniface's brother is spelled variously Bereharius, Bercharius, Barnharius, Bernhardus. See Simson, *op. cit.*, I, 299.

152. "et quosdam contigit oppetere." Cf. Vergil, *Aeneid*, I, 95f.: "Quis . . ./Contigit oppetere." See Manitius, "Zu dem Epos," 618.

153. I.e., on 1 July and 25 Dec., but according to Oppolzer, *op. cit.*, 356, one also occurred on 6 Jan. 828.

154. For a related bit of folklore about persons fallen from the sky, see Allen Cabaniss, "Agobard of Lyons: Rumour, Propaganda and Freedom of Thought in the Ninth Century," *History Today*, III, No. 2 (Feb. 1953), 128–34; reprinted as "Agobard of Lyons" in *Diversions of History*, ed. Peter Quennell (London: Allan Wingate, 1954), 41–51.

155. 28 Mar. 828, Easter.

156. 1 July 829.

157. For documentation, see Allen Cabaniss, *Agobard of Lyons: Churchman and Critic* (Syracuse: Syracuse University Press, 1953), 73.

158. St. Martin's day is 11 Nov.; St. Andrew's, 30 Nov.; Nativity, 25 Dec., of course; *cum reliquis* ("along with the rest") may refer to St. Stephen's (26 Dec.), St. John Evangelist's (27 Dec.), Holy Innocents' (28 Dec.), and possibly other days through Epiphany (6 Jan.).

PART III

1. Ash Wednesday, 1 Mar.—Easter, 17 April 830.

2. "factionis iniquae principes." Cf. *Annales regni Francorum, anno* 810: "huius factionis principes." See Manitius, "Zu deutschen Geschichtsquellen," 73.

3. This is apparently a proverbial statement, but I have been unable to trace it in exactly this form.

4. "quod dictu nefas sit." Cf. Cicero, *De senectute*, 5: "nefas esse dictu"; *Annales Fuldenses, anno* 878: "et quod dictu nefas est." See Manitius, "Zu deutschen Geschichtsquellen," 73.

5. Louis the Pious was Bernard's godfather, hence the use of the word *incestuous;* cf. Thegan, *Vita Ludovici imperatoris,* 36.

6. "quibusdam praestigiis elusum"—a suggestion of black magic and witchcraft believed by many of Louis's contemporaries. See below, notes 62, 170.

7. "hoc praetexentes nomine culpam." Cf. Vergil, *Aeneid,* IV, 172: "hoc praetexit nomine culpam." See Manitius, "Zu dem Epos," 618.

8. See chs. 41:1, 42:1 above. On Count Odo, a cousin of Bernard of Barcelona, see also chs. 45:1, 51:2, 52:2 and 52:3, below.

9. Somewhat ironic in view of Louis's two earlier "threats" to enter a monastery voluntarily; cf. chs. 19:1, 32:2 above.

10. This suggests that Lothair was not initially privy to the plan to replace his father, but see Nithard, *op. cit.,* I, *ad init.*

11. See Part II, note 83, above.

12. See note 8 above.

13. "infracti viribus." Cf. Vergil, *Aeneid,* IX, 499: "infractae ad proelia vires." See Manitius, "Zu dem Epos," 618.

14. "aut bello confligendum." Cf. Einhard, *Vita Karoli*, 15: "cum his namque bello conflixit." See Manitius, "Zu deutschen Geschichtsquellen," 72.

15. See Part II, note 81, above.

16. "iamdudum attonsos." In reality the time-element here was only about a year.

17. Other sources place the purgation after the second revolt of the sons, but this dating of it seems more logical.

18. 2 Feb. 831.

19. "cunctis diiudicatis ad mortem vitam concessit." Cf. Nithard, *De dissensionibus filiorum Ludovici pii*, I, 3: "et ab ipso Lodhario ad mortem diiudicati." See Manitius, "Zu deutschen Geschichtsquellen," 73.

20. Easter, 2 April 831; Ash Wednesday was 15 Feb.

21. Properly the Paschal season extends from Easter to Pentecost. In 831 the latter festival fell on 20 May.

22. Job 31:18 (Vulgate).

23. "sed ille . . . fugam capessit." Cf. Ammianus Marcellinus, *Rerum gestarum libri*, XVII, 8, 4: "nec fugam capessere." See Manitius, "Zu deutschen Geschichtsquellen," 71.

24. "hiemis . . . rigore peracto." Cf. Justin, *Historiarum ex Trogo Pompeio excerptarum libri*, II, 1: "hiemis rigore . . . secretam." See Manitius, "Zu deutschen Geschichtsquellen," 70.

25. 11 Nov. 832.

26. "humectationem terrae glaciali astringente rigore." Cf. *Annales Fuldenses*, anno 860: "mare etiam Ionium glaciali rigore ita constrictum est." See Manitius, "Zu deutschen Geschichts-quellen," 73.

27. "qui vectatione equorum uteretur" (literally, "who would resort to riding horses"). Cf. Suetonius, *Caligula*, 3: "repleta assidua equi vectatione." See Manitius, "Zu deutschen Geschichts-quellen," 70.

28. I Cor. 15:33. This iambic trimeter is cited by St. Paul from the pagan Menander's *Thais*.

29. A proverbial statement probably based on Ovid, *Epistolae*, IV, 10, 5: "Gutta cavat lapidem." See Nickel, *Untersuchungen*, 45.

30. According to *Annales Fuldenses* and *Bertiniani*, *anno* 833, and Thegan, *Vita Ludovici imperatoris*, 41, the date was Feb.; Thegan's notation being, "ante sanctum tempus quadragesimae," which began in that year on 16 Feb.

31. Thirtieth bishop of Strasbourg, 817—17 April 840; more usual spelling of the name is Bernald.

32. 24 June 833.

33. "ignominia notatus." Cf. Cicero, *Ad familiares*, VI, 6, 11: "nulla ignominia notati." The location is Rotfeld near Colmar. See Manitius, "Zu deutschen Geschichtsquellen," 71.

34. I.e., Louis charged that he simply treated Pope Gregory IV as the pope would have treated him had positions been reversed.

35. "inexorabili contra filios discordia laborare." Cf. Justin, *Historiarum ex Trogo Pompeio excerptarum libri*, IV, 3: "cum Rhegini discordia laborarent." See Manitius, "Zu deutschen Geschichtsquellen," 70.

36. 29 June 833.

37. Only our anonymous author gives the name of this city.

38. 1 Oct. 833.

39. A principle based ultimately on an interpretation of Nahum 1:9.

40. 11 Nov. 833.

41. Eggebard is mentioned again in ch. 50 below; and William, count of Blois, brother of Odo (see note 8 above), and thus cousin of Bernard of Barcelona, is mentioned again in ch. 52:3, below.

42. Illegitimate half-brother of Emperor Louis; see also chs. 51:2, 55:1, below.

43. Out of many such passages, I cite only this one to illustrate the rhetorical device of prose-rhyme:

> Suasionibus accendebant,
> promissionibus alliciebant,
> iuramentis astringebant,
> et in unum velle foederabant.

44. Ash Wednesday, 18 Feb. 834; Easter, 5 April.

45. The fifth feria of the first week of Lent, 834, was Thursday 19 Feb. On Atrebaldus, abbot of Flavigny, see chs. 55:2, 56, 59:1, below. Bernard of Barcelona had a brother named Gautselm; see also the Count Gotselinus mentioned in ch. 52:3, below.

46. On Guerinius, see Part II, note 80, above; on Odo, note 8 above; on Fulco, ch. 55:2, below; and on Hugo, note 42 above.

47. 1 Mar. 834.

48. The middle or fourth Sunday in Lent, 834, was 15 March. Also called "Laetare" Sunday from the first word of the Introit (quoted in the text above), it has many other names: Mothering, Refreshment (shared with third Sunday in Advent, from the Gospel of the day, the feeding of the five thousand), Simnel, Rose (from the color of the vestments), Jerusalem (from the Epistle of the day), New, Alb, etc.

49. Introit of Mass for fourth Sunday in Lent (see preceding note), based on Isa. 66:10. Observe that the author here used the word *officium* for what is customarily called in the Roman usage *introitus*. *Officium* was the word employed by the Mozarabic liturgy, and *ingressa* by the Ambrosian; both belonging to the general classification of Gallican rites.

50. All MSS read, "ibique Iudith Augustam ab Italia reducentibus Rataldo episcopo et Bonifacio sed et Pippinum filium recepit." *Pippinum* should nonetheless be emended to *Pippino*, in accordance with *Annales Bertiniani, anno* 834 (this Pepin being the son of the late King Bernard of Italy and a great-nephew of Emperor Louis). The word *filium* I have transferred to the following sentence as relating to young Charles (the Bald). On

Rataldus, see Part II, note 63, above; on Boniface, Part II, note 150, above. Consult Simson, *op. cit.*, II, 300.

51. 5 April 834.

52. 24 May 834.

53. "et alii multi imperatoris faventes partibus." Cf. Nithard, *op. cit.*, II, 3: "cum his qui parti suae favebant." See Manitius, "Zu deutschen Geschichtsquellen," 73.

54. "terga hostibus nudaverunt." Cf. Vergil, *Aeneid*, V, 586: "terga fuga nudant." See Manitius, "Zu dem Epos," 618.

55. "salutem in fugae subsidio posuere." Cf. Caesar, *Bellum Gallicum*, II, 11: "Omnes in fuga sibi praesidium posuere." See Manitius, "Zu deutschen Geschichtsquellen," 70.

56. "ad Lotharium quantocius mittunt ut sibi suppeditaretur quos tanti discriminis circumvallaret metus; qui audito eorum periculo et rebus gestis eis deliberavit succurrere." Cf. Nithard, *op. cit.*, I, 5: "quod quidem citato cursu victores Lothario notantes mandant ut quantocius posset illis cum exercitu occurrat qui libenter paruit." See Nickel, *Untersuchungen*, 20f.

57. "si aliquid ab adversarum partium studiosis moliretur novi." Cf. Suetonius, *Tiberius*, 11: "et quasi studiosiorem partis alterius." See Manitius, "Zu deutschen Geschichtsquellen," 70.

58. "quae in circuitu civitatis erant incendio conflagrata sunt." Cf. Einhard, *op. cit.*, 17: "qui tamen . . . incendio conflagravit." See Manitius, "Zu deutschen Geschichtsquellen," 72.

59. Other sources say *three* days. See, e.g., Nithard, *op. cit.*, I, 5.

60. "lambentibus flammis." Cf. Vergil, Aeneid, II, 684: "lambere flamma comas." See Manitius, "Zu dem Epos," 618.

61. On Gotselinus, see note 45 above; on Sanila, Part II, note 86, above. Madalelm is mentioned only here in this *Vita*.

62. "tanquam venefica." Cf. note 6 above. As a daughter of Count William, she was a sister of Bernard of Barcelona.

63. "Lingonum civitatem." I.e., Langres.

64. "in villam cuius vocabulum est Matualis." Tentatively identified as Laval or St. Calais (dép. Sarthe).

65. 11 Nov. 835.

66. This person may or may not be identified with Ermoldus Nigellus, author of the four books of elegiacs on the life of Louis the Pious, on whom see the introduction to Ermold le Noir, *Poème sur Louis le Pieux et Épitres au Roi Pépin*, ed. and trans. Edmond Faral.

67. From this point through ch. 61, the author's chronology becomes exceedingly tangled. This is the first error: the diet was held, not at Worms, but at Crémieux (see *Annales Bertiniani, anno* 835), although our author maintains his insistence that it was at Worms in the following chapter. See Simson, *op. cit.*, II, 139.

68. Not at Aachen, but at Thionville; see *Annales Bertiniani, anno* 834.

69. The Christmas referred to was that of 834; the Purification, 2 Feb. 835.

70. This suggests that a bishop had to be present and that he had to declare himself unworthy.

71. See Cabaniss, *Agobard of Lyons: Churchman and Critic.*

72. Lent of 835 began on Ash Wednesday, 3 March; this date therefore is 28 Feb. 835.

73. Ash Wednesday, 3 March 835.

74. Easter, 18 April 835.

75. Pentecost, 6 June 835.

76. Not at Worms, but at Crémieux; see note 67 above.

77. I.e., after the Easter of 836, 9 April.

78. I.e., the winter of 835–836.

79. I.e., at Thionville, as noted in the preceding chapter.

80. I.e., after Easter, 9 April 836, as noted in the preceding chapter; *Annales Bertiniani, anno* 836, say *mense Maio*.

81. I.e., that Lothair should be present at a diet to be held at Worms in September 836.

82. Wala died on 31 Aug. or 12 Sept. 836. See Simson, *op. cit.*, II, 156f.

83. Cf. II Sam. 19:1–4.

84. To this point the author still has reference to matters of the year 836.

85. "The emperor also ordered . . . the emperor's will and other matters." The author is here referring to events during and after the council at Thionville in May 837; *Annales Bertiniani, anno* 837.

86. "But Lothair . . . could not save them." These two sentences revert to 836; *Annales Bertiniani, anno* 836.

87. To this point this sentence apparently refers to events of 837; but see the following note.

88. This part of the sentence relates to the emperor's activities near the end of 836; *Annales Bertiniani, anno* 836 .

89. With this paragraph the author again refers to 837.

90. This incident has the ring of "cloak-and-dagger" mystery. Is it possible that the "beggar" was our author?

91. 1 Sept.—11 Nov. 837; but the statement is not entirely accurate (see several following notes).

92. According to Gams, *op. cit.*, 487, and Duchesne, *op. cit.*, III, 129, Jesse, bishop of Amiens since 799, died in Aug. or Sept. 836.

93. According to Gams, *op. cit.*, 643, and Duchesne, *op. cit.*, II, 456, Helias, bishop of Troyes since 829, died in Aug. or Sept. 836.

94. Wala's death, 31 Aug. or 12 Sept. 836, has already been recorded above in ch. 55:1; see note 82 above.

95. According to *Annales Bertiniani, anno* 837, both Hugo and Lambert died in 837. I have not verified from other sources the dates on which Matfrid, Godefrid, Godefrid the younger, Agimbert, and Burgaret died.

96. "non post multum et ipse moritur." This is strange and confused language. This Richard died in Nov. 842; see Part I,

note 44, above. Incidentally, this date gives us the *terminus a quo* for the writing of this *Vita*.

97. Jer. 9:23.

98. "sed pugno pectore tunso." Cf. Vergil, *Aeneid*, I, 481: "et tunsae pectora palmis." See Manitius, "Zu dem Epos," 618.

99. Luke 18:13.

100. Wisd. 12:18. To this point (with exceptions specified above) our author seems to be dealing with the year 837.

101. Now he reverts to the year 836.

102. 2 Feb. 836, but it was really 6 Feb. 836; see Simson, *op. cit.*, II, 148.

103. Now at last the author comes to the assembly held at Crémieux in June 835; *Annales Bertiniani, anno* 835.

104. "in loco qui vocatur Stramiacus." Ordinarily interpreted as Crémieux, but some have held it to be Tramoyes. See G. Waitz, ed., *Annales Bertiniani* ("Scriptores rerum Germanicarum in usum scholarum"; Hannover: Hahn, 1883), 11, n. 3.

105. "res imperfecta remansit." Cf. Vergil, *Aeneid*, VIII, 458: "par imperfecta manebat." See Manitius, "Zu dem Epos," 618.

106. On this, see an important note in Simson, *op. cit.*, II, 300.

107. 11 Nov. 835.

108. This is the Christmas of 835.

109. This is the Easter of 836, 9 April.

110. This means the Paschal season of 837. The Lenten period was from Ash Wednesday, 14 Feb., to Easter, 1 April; and the Easter season, from Easter to Pentecost, 20 May. Technically only the latter period is the Paschal season, but our author may have included Lent by a kind of loose terminology.

111. This is an apparition of Halley's comet. See F. Baldet and G. de Obaldia, *Catalogue général des orbites de comètes de l'an −466 à 1952* (Paris: Centre National de la Recherche Scientifique, 1952), 10, 53, 59, which gives the perihelion date as 1 March

and the duration of observation as 22 March—28 April 837. See also D. J. Schove, "Halley's Comet, I: 1930 B.C. to A.D. 1896," *Journal of the British Astronomical Association*, LXV, No. 7 (July 1955), 285–89; Michael Kamienski, "Halley's Comet and Early Chronology," *ibid.*, LXVI, No. 4 (March 1956), 127–31; Kamienski, "The Probable Apparition of Halley's Comet in 2320 B.C.," *Acta Astronomica*, VI, No. 1 (1956), 3–23; Kamienski, "Researches on the Periodicity of Halley's Comet, Part III: Revised List of Ancient Perihelion Passages of the Comet," *ibid.*, VII, No. 2 (1957), 111–18. *Serpens* (the Serpent) and *Corvus* (the Crow or Raven) are, of course, constellations.

I am greatly indebted to my dean, Professor A. B. Lewis, Department of Physics and Astronomy, the University of Mississippi, for working with me on this problem. I am also indebted to Janice S. Brown, Chief, Reference and Circulation, Smithsonian Institution, and Hélène M. Gingras, Assistant Librarian, United States Naval Observatory, Washington, D.C., for assisting me with a bibliography of the comet.

112. "non more errantium septem siderum orientem versus peteret." Certainly ambiguous, but probably rendered as above; otherwise how account for the phrase, "quod mirum est dictu" (which is marvelous to relate)?

113. Note that the movement through the zodiacal signs (constellations) is *retrograde:* Virgo, Leo, Cancer, Gemini.

114. Here the comet appears fixed because it is moving toward aphelion.

115. A very important indication of the self-consciousness and pride of the author as well as his intimacy at court.

116. Cf. Col. 4:5, Eph. 5:16.

117. Jer. 10:2 (differs verbally from the Vulgate).

118. "noctemque illam . . . pervigilem." Cf. Justin, *op. cit.*, XII, 13: "noctem pervigilem iunxisset." See Manitius, "Zu deutschen Geschichtsquellen," 70.

119. Cf. Adolph Franz, *Die Messe im Deutschen Mittelalter* (Freiburg i/B: Herder, 1902), 73–154 and *passim.*

120. "sed quia inofficiosa remansit."

121. Cf. *Annales Bertiniani, anno* 837.

122. Early in 838; *Annales Bertiniani, anno* 838.

123. According to *Annales Bertiniani, anno* 838, it was in mid-August, but mid-September seems more likely.

124. At Ver; cf. *Annales Bertiniani, anno* 838.

125. Not at Aachen, but at Mainz; *Annales Bertiniani* and *Fuldenses, anno* 838.

126. 1 Jan., but of what year? The text would ordinarily suggest 839, but that is contradicted by the following sentence (the death of Pepin which occurred on 13 Dec. 838). See Simson, *op. cit.*, II, 191–94. The comet does not help our chronology because no comet of this date is listed in the works mentioned in note 111 above. On the other hand, the year 837 was "a remarkable one for such bodies," since Chinese records mention four; C. P. Oliver, *Comets* (Baltimore: Williams and Wilkins Co., 1930), 105. It may therefore be that this is a misplaced allusion to Halley's comet of 837. See the following note.

127. As indicated in the preceding note, Pepin died on 13 Dec. 838; *Annales Bertiniani, anno* 838, and in part *Annales Fuldenses, anno* 838 (with minor inaccuracies). The phrase, "non multo post" (soon after), indicates how vague and erratic the author's chronology is at this point.

128. This plan is adverted to first in ch. 54:3 above. Observe that this sentence apparently refers to the year 839; see the following note.

129. Easter, 6 April 839. Lothair came in May and left in July; *Annales Fuldenses* and *Bertiniani, anno* 839.

130. I.e., either the emperor and young Charles would suggest the division and Lothair would be allowed to assign the portions

or Lothair would suggest the division and the emperor and Charles would make the assignments. Cf. Nithard, *op. cit.*, I, *ad fin.*: "Hinc pater ut sui iuraverant perficere cupiens: 'Ecce, fili, ut promiseram regnum omne coram te est; divide illud prout libuerit. Quod si tu diviseris, partium electio Caroli erit. Si autem nos illud diviserimus, similiter partium electio tua erit.'"

131. The emperor spent Christmas 839, not at Aix, but at Poitiers; *Annales Bertiniani, anno* 839. See Simson, *op. cit.*, II, 220f.

132. He did spend Easter, 28 March 840, at Aix, having left Judith and young Charles in Poitiers; *Annales Bertiniani, anno* 840.

133. Here is an apparent confusion. Louis of Bavaria was in reality protesting the "secret" plan of 837 (mentioned at the beginning of ch. 59 above), about which he and Lothair had held their "secret" meeting in Italy early in 838 (also mentioned at the beginning of ch. 59 above). Louis made this protest at the assembly at Nijmegen in May or June 838 and hence before the autumn assembly at Kierzy mentioned early in ch. 59 above; *Annales Bertiniani* (May) and *Fuldenses* (June), *anno* 838, and see the following note for further evidence of date.

134. "quicquid regni trans Rhenum fuit sibi vindicandum statuit." Cf. Nithard, *op. cit.*, I, 6: "quicquid trans Rhenum regni continebatur sibi vindicare vellet." See also the similar words in *Annales Bertiniani, anno* 838: "Hlodowicus autem patris praesentiae secundum quod iussum fuerat sese offerre non distulit, habitaque secus quam oportuerat conflictatione verborum, quicquid ultra citraque Renum paterni iuris usurpaverat, recipiente patre, amisit. . . ."

135. "he judged . . . was finished, however." These phrases presumably refer to the year 840 (see note 129 above); *Annales Bertiniani* and *Fuldenses, anno* 840.

136. "deeming that . . . left him in his own domain." Re-

ferring to events of 839: the emperor crossed the Rhine on 7 Jan. 839, spent Lent at Frankfurt and Easter (6 April 839) at Bodman; *Annales Bertiniani* and *Fuldenses, anno* 839.

137. "Rhenum quidem apud Moguntiacum transiit et Triburas venit." Probably to be emended to "Rhenum quidem Mogunumque (or, Mogumque) transiit." See Simson, *op. cit.*, II, 300.

138. Between the events of this and the following paragraphs Louis the Pious was at Ingelheim on 18 May 839 (*Annales Bertiniani, anno* 839), at Worms (see ch. 60 above), and at Kreuznach (*Annales Bertiniani, anno* 839).

139. The hunt in the Ardennes is mentioned in *Annales Bertiniani, anno* 839, as taking place in the summer of 839.

140. Ebroin had apparently just been made bishop. Later the archchaplain of Charles the Bald, he died on 18 April 858; see L. Levillain, "L'archichapelain Ebroin, évêque de Poitiers," *Moyen Age*, XXXIV (1923), 177–215; also Buchner, "Enstehungszeit." On Reginard, see Part II, note 67, above. Gerard and Ratharius are mentioned only here in this *Vita*.

141. The MSS read *fratrem* or *patrem*, either of which is an error since his *brother* Pepin was king of Italy and his *father* was Charles. Hence the reading should be *filium* or *nepotem* (grandson). I adopt *nepotem* because of the context.

142. The words of Herod the Great appearing in the Latin translation by Rufinus of Flavius Josephus, *De bello Iudaico*, I, 17; in the 1528 edition published at Lyons by Sebastianus Gryphis, this occurs on p. 82. I am indebted for verification of this to Miss Mahala Saville, Reference Librarian of the University of Mississippi, and Mrs. Helen Wooley, Assistant in the Rare Book Room of the University of Illinois Library.

143. On 1 Sept. 839; *Annales Bertiniani, anno* 839.

144. Confirmed by *Annales Bertiniani, anno* 839.

145. The emperor was in Poitiers on Epiphany (6 Jan.) 840, and on Purification (2 Feb.) 840; *Annales Bertiniani, anno* 840.

Assistance in translating the medical terminology following has been kindly given me by Dean D. S. Pancratz, Director of the University of Mississippi Medical Center, Jackson, and Mrs. Pancratz.

146. Judith and young Charles remained in Poitiers after the emperor left; *Annales Bertiniani, anno* 840.

147. Ash Wednesday occurred on 10 Feb. 840.

148. Cf. John 10:11.

149. Cf. I Pet. 5:4.

150. Easter, 28 March 840; see also ch. 60 above, last sentence.

151. For confirmation, see *Annales Bertiniani* and *Fuldenses, anno* 840.

152. This sentence is in error. Judith and young Charles had not accompanied him; see note 146 above.

153. The three days before Ascension Thursday are called Rogation days or the Major Litany. In 840 Ascension day was 6 May; the eclipse occurred therefore on 5 May 840, the date confirmed by Oppolzer, *op. cit.*, 196. See Simson, *op. cit.*, II, 226.

154. This is an excellent description of a total eclipse of the sun.

155. "singultibus quati." Cf. Sedulius, *Carmen paschale*, III, 107: "vix verba precantia fari / Singultu quatiente valens."

156. See also *Annales Bertiniani* and *Fuldenses, anno* 840, for confirmation.

157. Hethi (Hetti, Hetto), successor of Amalarius, bishop from 816 or 819 until his death on 27 May 847; see Duchesne, *op. cit.*, III, 42.

158. Bishop, 826 to death, 21 June 847; predecessor of Rabanus Maurus. On Drogo, see Part II, note 109, above.

159. Cf. Ps. 51:17 (Vulgate, 50:19).

160. Cf. Ps. 119–37 (Vulgate, 118:137); Jer. 12:1; Rev. 16:5, 7; 19:2.

161. "grates persolverent." Cf. Vergil, *Aeneid*, II, 537: "per-

solvant grates dignas." See Manitius, "Zu dem Epos," 618.

162. "quem chorus virtutum semper comitatus fuerat." Cf. Vergil, *Georgics*, I, 346: "omnis quam chorus et socii comitentur ovantes." See Manitius, "Zu dem Epos," 618.

163. Rom. 12:1.

164. Evening and night of Saturday, 19 June 840.

165. Usually called Matins today, the very early morning service.

166. "pectus suum muniretur." Cf. Einhard, *op. cit.*, 23: "umeros ac pectus hieme muniebat." See Manitius, "Zu deutschen Geschichtsquellen," 72.

167. Emending *ligno* to the obvious *signo*. See Simson, *op. cit.*, II, 300.

168. I.e., Sunday, 20 June 840.

169. The rite called "the Commendation of a Soul."

170. An interesting allusion to witchcraft; see note 6 above.

171. An exceedingly ironic remark, for if it is true it means that the only time in his life that Louis ever laughed was here at the end of his life, Thegan, *op. cit.*, 19, being our witness that "he never showed his white teeth in laughter." See Part II, note 45, above. There is a curious parallel to this death-bed scene in Erasmus, *Apotheosis Capnionis* (his dialogue on the reception of Reuchlin among the saints), but it is no doubt only an apparent reminiscence.

172. I have tried in vain to track down this exact quotation. Statements like this are, of course, commonplace and may be found in Seneca, Cicero, St. Augustine, St. Isidore, *et al*. What makes this so tantalizing is the assertion that it was made "a veridico doctore." A query in *Notes and Queries*, n.s., V, No. 7 (July 1958), 321, has not elicited a reply.

173. I.e., on 20 June.

174. Nithard, *op. cit.*, I, *ad fin.*, records virtually the same statement: "vixit per annos sexaginta quatuor. Rexit Aquitaniam per annos triginta septem. Imperiale vero nomen per annos viginti

septem et per menses sex obtinuit." Louis was king of Aquitaine at his birth in early summer or late spring of 778 (see ch. 3 above) and became emperor at the death of his father, 28 Jan. 814; counting both 778 and 814, as was customary, this makes thirty-seven years. He was emperor from the death of his father until his own death here recorded; counting similarly this makes twenty-seven years. Evidence for this method of counting is obvious from Nithard's remark, "et per menses sex," for it is only by including January through June that we get the six months. It is then by adding the thirty-seven years of kingship and the twenty-seven years of emperorhood that our author arrives at "the sixty-fourth year of his life." By his own method of computation, i.e., by adding both *terminus a quo* and *terminus ad quem*, it should have been the sixty-third; by ours it would be for practical purposes exactly the sixty-second. In any case the year 840 and the date 20 June are confirmed by *Annales Bertiniani* and *Fuldenses, anno* 840, as well as by other sources.

175. Not a part of the original text but added in some MSS.

Index of Proper Names in the Text